Love and Justice

A Workbook for Christian Moral Awareness

Student Book

William J. O'Malley, S.J.

After eighty years of modern social teachings and over two thousand years of the gospel of love, the church has to admit her inability to make more impact on the conscience of her people. The faithful, particularly the more wealthy and comfortable, simply do not see structured social injustice as a sin, and they feel no personal responsibility for it. To live like Dives with Lazarus at the gate is not even perceived to be sinful.

—*The Roman Synod, 1971*

Loyola University Press—Chicago, Illinois

Loyola University Press
3441 North Ashland
Chicago, Illinois 60657

Design by J.L. Boden
Acknowledgements:
Illustrations on pages 7, 17, 20, 28, 40, 80, 94, 15,
123, 128 by Geoffrey Moss
©1975, Washington Post Writers Group,
reprinted with permission

Library of Congress Cataloging in Publication Data

O'Malley, William J.
   Love and justice.

   1. Christianity and justice.   I. Title.
   BR115.J8043   1985   241   85-9
   ISBN 0-8294-0482-1

This book is for
Larry Wroblewski, S.J.
and for Jean Cardinali
who make everything easier.

Contents

Part I: The Principles of Justice

Part II: The Practice of Justice

Introduction

This book is divided into two parts: Part I, The Principles of Justice, and Part II, the Practice of Justice.

The first part is meant to establish just what justice means, so that we all understand each other and don't go off half-cocked and miss one another in the dark. It begins independently of any religion, working simply from reason, since justice is not "Christian." All human beings, regardless of their religious beliefs or lack of them, are called to do justice by their very human nature and by the need we all have to live together and not alone.

Therefore, this book first studies what being human means, and it shows how the need for justice rises just as inevitably out of human nature as an oak rises from an acorn. Conscience is as natural to us as thinking and loving and wanting to grow. But there are obstacles. Human beings—and therefore human consciences—are imperfect. Selfishness can very often blind us to the truth and, in doing untruth, we automatically do injustice. But consciences can grow.

Moreover, we don't live alone. We band together, not only because we get lonely by ourselves, but because a group can accomplish what an individual or even many disconnected individuals cannot. But since groups are made up of imperfect human beings, groups can also create injustice. Therefore, the last three chapters of Part I deal with how three different sciences cope with our living together: economics, politics, and religion.

Part II considers particular injustices which occur when two sets of rights (or what people consider to be their rights) come into conflict: war, capital punishment, abortion, euthanasia, racism, sexism, and poverty.

Be warned here at the beginning about two paralyzing responses to these considerations: guilt and burn-out.

If the questions and considerations on these pages only make you feel guilty, they will have failed. Guilt is sick—unless it turns into reasoned responsibility. Note: "reasoned" responsibility. You have only about sixteen waking hours a day, and there are many people who have claims on your attention and effort. You can't help every cripple in the world. But you can help some.

If these pages make you so aware of human suffering that they become discouraging, they will also have failed. It can be a harrowing experience suddenly to become aware of the enormity of the world's injustices. There will likely be times when you will say, "Look. Enough! No, too much." Once again remember that you can't heal all the wounds, but you can heal some. This book is a sweep over the whole field–so that you can decide which wounds you personally might be best equipped to heal.

Don't underestimate your power. If you are able to reach out and cure one person's shyness, the sum of human pain will be that much less. And if we can all get together, we can make a noise that will make the world sit up and take notice. We may not make people change much, but we can make them very, very uncomfortable.

By your birth, you were commissioned to act as a truly human being; you were missioned to justice. By your baptism, you were ordained an apostle, a prophet; you were missioned to love.

It's time we all got about our task. It's time we all laid claim to our birthright: the sons and daughters of The Most High.

William J. O'Malley, S.J.
Rochester, New York

Part I
The Principles of Justice

Unit 1

All Men (and Women) Are Created Equal

All animals are equal . . . but some animals
are more equal than others.
—George Orwell

Clinton, Virginia: Ev Slocum runs a nice little filling station and auto repair shop. Business is good. People around Clinton like Ev. What's better, they trust him. In May he put an ad in the paper for a youngster to help out after school, Saturdays, and during the summer—not just pumping gas but working the grease pit, too. Ev got three responses the first day.

The first was Tommy Clarke, smart kid, top of his class over at the high school. Bit spindly, though, and didn't know a carburetor from a hubcap. When Ev asked why such a rich boy wanted such a job, Tommy laughed and said his father had told him that if he wanted a motorcycle, he'd have to pay for it himself.

The second was Peggy Washburn, known to her less kindly schoolmates as "Miss Piggy." Her brother had taught her a lot about engines, but Peggy had a mouth on her that would make a Marine wince. Still, surprisingly, she broke down crying and said she needed the money for tuition. Ev wasn't so sure

that his customers would go for a girl working on the innards of their cars.

The final kid was Cleavon Morris who'd worked in a machine shop till it folded. Cleavon was a very big boy and very quick with his hands. When Ev asked why he wanted the job, Cleavon sort of hemmed and hawed and finally told him that the whole family had to work to make up his father's bail money. Ev himself wasn't very partial to "colored folks."

Ev was left with a pretty tough decision.

Amazonia, Brazil: Taureg did not know that the year was 1985. But he did know that, with his wife and children and his wife's mother, he was probably the last of the Cintas Largas tribe of Indians left alive. For generations his people had retreated further and further into the jungle, away from the monstrous machines that sheared off his wife's small plot

of manioc and his carefully built straw hut. The machines belched smoke and noise and mangled down the brush and the great rubber trees and huge rocks, scarring the jungle with red-brown roads and the poles with the singing wires.

Whole villages had perished overnight when they ate the food dropped from the loud steel birds by the white men. Hundreds had been poisoned, too, by the white man's diseases: syphilis, tuberculosis, even ordinary head colds, for which the Indians had never had to develop an immunity.

The Indian agent from Brasilia had explained very patiently that this was for "The National Progress," but Taureg did not know what that meant. It was not "progress" for him and his family. Finally, the white men had come with the sticks that belch fire and send metal through a man's flesh. The Indians had fled. Now there was nowhere left to flee. And, once again, Taureg heard the great machines in the distance, coming closer.

3

Taureg made a vow. He was going to kill the white men.

———————

Mid-Atlantic: The Finnish liner, Sibelius, had been driven many miles off course by the storm and had struck an iceberg. Finally, a bit past midnight, the ship slowly heeled over, and, with a terrifying hiss, gradually disappeared beneath the murky waters.

The ten-foot waves had driven the tiny lifeboats miles apart, and, in the darkness, they were completely isolated from one another. It was as if each one was all alone on the face of the immense sea. In Lifeboat #26, which was built for six, there were twelve people, some crammed into the tiny shell, some clinging to the sides in the icy water. The experienced crewman aboard estimated that, since they were so far off course, and since the storm was likely to last at least another day, it would be days before they were likely to be found. In the panic to get aboard, half the rations and most of the water had been lost into the sea. He estimated that they had enough water to last three people two days; with rigid rationing, perhaps six people.

Besides the crewman, there were: a Nobel chemist, a pregnant woman, a bishop, a college professor of Shakespeare, an Olympic diver, a very wealthy shoe manufacturer and his crippled wife, a mechanic, a film star, her senator husband and their retarded seventeen-year-old daughter. If any of them were to survive, six people would have to go, voluntarily or not. The crewman had a pistol. He also had a very big decision on his hands.

———————————————

Pre-Test

Circle the letter of the answer which you personally believe is closest to the truth.

1. Ev Slocum should have hired: (A) Tommy Clarke; (B) Peggy Washburn;   (C) Cleavon Morris;   (D) an adult.

2. Taureg: (A) would have been justified in killing at least one of the white intruders;   (B) would have been justified in killing the foreman;   (C) would have been justified in destroying the intruders' machines;   (D) should have bowed to the inevitable.

3. What percentage of poor people in the United States who are capable of working actually do work year-round and are still poor? (A) 30%;   (B) 50%;   (C) 60%;   (D) 95%.

4. Which group has the highest level of poverty?   (A) Blacks; (B) American Indians;   (C) Hispanics;   (D) Whites.

5. According to experts, what is the greatest problem facing the poor today: (A) lack of opportunity;   (B) poor schools;   (C) food costs;   (D) laziness.

6. Of all Americans at this time, what percentage are functionally illiterate; that is, they can barely get by with reading and writing? (A) 10%;   (B) 20%;   (C) 25%;   (D) 30%.

7. Of all the wealth in the United States, the richest 20% of the people own: (A) 20%;   (B) 30%;   (C) 40%;   (D) 50%.

8. Of all the wealth in the United States, the poorest 20% of the people own: (A) 5%;   (B) 10%;   (C) 20%;   (D) 30%.

9. The majority of the people who get government assistance (Welfare, etc.) are: (A) Blacks;   (B) Hispanics;   (C) Indians; (D) children.

10. If the head of the family earns $10,000 a year, about how much can a family of four spend on food per person, per day?   (A) $2.05; (B) $5.18;   (C) $7.56;   (D) $10.34.

The Sibelius Quandary

Choose the people who will stay and who will have to go from the Sibelius lifeboat. "1" indicates your first choice to stay; "12" indicates your first choice to go.

	After Reading	After Discussing	After Role-play
Crewman			
Nobel chemist			
Pregnant woman			
Bishop			
Shakespeare prof			
Olympic diver			
Shoe manufacturer			
Crippled wife			
Mechanic			
Film star			
Senator husband			
Retarded daughter			

The Weird Monopoly Qualifier

Fill in the blanks; then add up your own total score:

1. *Height* Males: + 5 for each inch over 5'7", − 5 for each inch under 5'7"; Females: + 10 if you are 5'7", − 5 for each inch over or under 5'7".

1._____

2. *Weight* Using the chart below, check the proper weight for a person of your height and sex. If you are exactly right: + 10. If you are over or under, − 1 for each pound.

2._____

3. *Body* Athletic: + 20; Average: 0; Too thin: − 10; Too heavy: − 20.

3._____

4. *Hair* Blond(e): + 10; Red: + 5; Brown: 0; Grey: − 10; Balding: − 20.

4._____

5. *Skin* Tanned: + 15; Pink: + 10; Freckled: + 5; Acne: − 5; Yellow: − 10; Brown: − 15; Black: − 20; Red: − 25.

5._____

6. *Overall Looks* Complimented often: + 20; Complimented sometimes: + 10; Complimented once or twice: + 5; Never complimented: − 10; Sometimes laughed at: − 20; Frequently laughed at: − 30.

6._____

7. *Income* Even if you are unsure of your parents' income, take a guess. For each $1,000 they make yearly over $20,000, + 5; for each $1,000 under $20,000, − 5.

7._____

8. *Parents Education* For each parent, Doctorate: + 50; Masters: + 30; College: + 20; High school: + 10.

8._____

9. *Neighborhood* Affluent: + 30; Ordinary: + 10; Poor: − 10; Ghetto: − 20.

9._____

10. *Academic Potential* Add your combined PSAT score or one-tenth your SAT score.

10._____

TOTAL SCORE[1]   _____

---

[1]All those who said somewhere along the line. "This isn't fair," were absolutely right.

Ideal weight in pounds by height:

For males:

4'8"	112	5'4"	128-135	5'10"	150-158
5'0"	116-125	5'6"	135-142	6'0"	158-167
5'2"	121-130	5'8"	142-150	6'2"	165-178

For females:

4'9"	99-108	5'2"	108-121	5'8"	126-139
4'11"	101-112	5'4"	114-127	5'10"	132-145
5'0"	103-115	5'6"	120-133	6'0"	138-151

Role-Play

The Ramseys have two children. Todd, 17, is a young man of startling good looks: long-lashed eyes, a tousled shock of wavy blond hair, and a body lean as steel from working his way up to captain of the swim team in his junior year. His name is scratched into desks all over St. Ursula's Academy. As if that weren't enough, he is also a National Merit Semi-Finalist, though he probably won't become a finalist, since his father makes over $75,000 a year.

Jimmy, the younger boy, is a sophomore and in constant trouble. He was suspended once when he was caught smoking pot at a school dance. His parents are worried about the group he hangs around with, mostly well-to-do, well-mannered with adults, but inclined to take too many risks, like drinking then driving. In school, Jimmy "coasts." His teachers say he might be as bright as his older brother, but he never takes a book home. June exams are over, and the principal has called in the Ramseys to see if Jimmy "wouldn't be happier somewhere else."

Role-Play
 —Jimmy with either of his parents
 —Jimmy with Todd
 —Jimmy with his counselor

Notebook Question

Page 1: The United States was founded on the principle that all men (and women) were created equal. But, as George Orwell says, "All animals are equal, but some animals are *more* equal than others." (A) In what ways, if any, do you feel, "more equal" than than most people in this country and/or this world? (B) In what ways, if any, do you feel "less equal"?

Meditation

God put all the separate parts into the body on purpose. If all the parts were the same, how could it be a body? As it is, the parts are many, but the body is one. The eye cannot say to the hand, "I don't need you," nor can the hand say to the feet, "I don't need you." What is more, it is precisely the parts of the body that seem to be the weakest which are the indispensible ones.

—I Corinthians 12:18-22

While an enormous mass of people still lack the absolute necessities of life, some, even in less advanced countries, live sumptuously and squander wealth. Luxury and misery rub shoulders. While the few enjoy very great freedom of choice, the many are deprived of almost all possibility of acting on their own initiative and responsibility, and often subsist in living and working conditions unworthy of human beings.

—Vatican II, The Church Today

Unit 2

Mommy, Where Do Consciences Come From?

"It ain't bad people that raises hell. It's dumb ones."
—John Steinbeck

Seattle, Washington: The senior girls at Queen of Peace High decided to stage a senior prank the night before the Senior Prom. It would be their last real time together—not as formal ladies crossing a stage to grab a piece of paper and a rose, but as friends. Beth O'Connor, the "doer" of her class, managed to sign up eighty girls—half the class, a real cross section of brains and jocks, "ladies" and "toughs," "ins" and "outs."

They agreed to meet at 10 p.m. at Fritz's (a beer joint with apparent police immunity), have a few beers, and with a school key Beth had had all year long, break into school with sleeping bags for an overnight. There were only three requirements: girls only, no beer in the school itself, and a blood oath not to tell the nuns. For a while, it was wonderful. A tiny bit sauced, they giggled into the basement corridor farthest from the convent and lay in the dark gossiping till 1 a.m.

Then it got a bit much. Some wanted to sleep, but the others wouldn't shut up. So a few locked themselves in the newspaper office. At 2 a.m. there was a fire extinguisher war. At 3 a.m. four girls broke into the cafeteria and raided the ice boxes. By 5 a.m. all but six had gone home. The bill for broken locks, ice cream, and refilling the extinguishers came to $183.45. Nobody came forward to take the blame or to accuse anyone else, because of their oath. So Sister Therese, the principal, added two dollars to the cost of each of the senior prom tickets. The girls in the newspaper office had slept through the whole ruckus. Many of the girls who went to the prom hadn't even been in school that night.

St. Louis, Missouri: Marion Rogers had three sons. Mike, 15, had a temper; and every time his mother asked him to mow the lawn, he looked as if he were ready to explode. He came about as close to swearing at his mother as he could and, invariably, stalked out of the house. Strong mea-sures from his father didn't seem to work. Tom, 14, had a touch of the same temper. He didn't say much, but his female parent was well aware that, even while he was trundling the mower out of the garage, she was being "told," and that he'd grump for three days. But whenever Larry, 12, came home from eighth grade, he'd pop in the door and say, "Hi, Mom, anything you want me to do before the ballgame?"

It's a bitter day in January. Marion has a cold, and she's wondering which of the boys she should ask to shovel the walk.

Your Town: It's eight o'clock on a Monday morning. You're washing the dishes when the doorbell rings. You dry your hands and open the door.

"Good morning," says the bright-eyed young man in the doorway. "This is your eviction notice."

You laugh for a minute. Then

10

stop. "What is this?" The young man smiles and says, "We got no desire to upset you. You certainly musta heard. Oil's been discovered under this whole block, high-grade stuff, seems like it goes all the way downta China!" He laughs.

"Now wait just one minute...."

"Look. The government's given us the right of eminent domain. We can offer you 50 cents on the dollar for your land and your house. We can't offer more. We gotta pay to bulldoze the houses outta here."

Understandably, you lean against the door. "This is unheard of," you wail, certain that it's a nightmare.

"Whaddya mean? We did it to the Oakies in Oklahoma in the thirties. We been doin' it to the Indians for five hundred years. An' they didn't get nuthin' at all. Consider yourself luckier. You got a week to get out."

Pre-Test

Judge whether each of the following is fair or unfair.

1. Sister Therese spread the cost of breakage among all the seniors.　　Fair　　Unfair

2. Marion Rogers asked her youngest son Larry to shovel the walk.　　Fair　　Unfair

3. In the interests of the common good, the government has the right to evict you from your home, as long as it gives you the compensation it judges to be fair.　　Fair　　Unfair

4. The Dutch paid $24 in beads for Manhattan Island, and the Indians were willing to accept it.　　Fair　　Unfair

5. "Wait a minute! I was here first!"　　Fair　　Unfair

6. Teachers are rightly expected to come to class prepared. If they don't, they should be disciplined and finally fired if they refuse to improve.　　Fair　　Unfair

7. Students are only young once. It is unreasonable to expect them to come to class every day prepared.　　Fair　　Unfair

8. Perhaps he's not as qualified as the other applicants, but after all he is my son-in-law.　　Fair　　Unfair

9. Perhaps he's not as qualified as the other applicants, but after all he's black; and somebody has to start giving them a break.   Fair   Unfair

10. "Aw, honey, you've *got* to let me! I took you out for dinner. And we've . . . been going together for two years. And you let me go this far. Don't you love me at all?   Fair   Unfair

---

Some Opinions on Conscience

Socialization. One's opinions of right and wrong are gradually assimilated from watching other people, observing what actions get punished and what actions are rewarded. Over the course of time, people have observed what actions are beneficial and what actions are harmful to the common good. They framed laws and, even though society seldom rewards the good, it will quite often punish the nonconformist.

In more primitive societies, socialization was a process of learning the tribal customs, particularly its taboos. In modern times, this process begins with the mother, continues with the school system, and then is taken over by the civil authority, one's spouse, and one's employer. Therefore, as Dr. B. F. Skinner asserts, the individual is solely the result of his or her conditioning.

Individual Choice. Morality is up to the individual. An action is all right provided no one else is hurt. No absolute rules can envision the unique complexities of each individual case. Only the individual in the particular situation can judge that. Just as the customs of different societies differ—and differ even within the same society over a period of time—the moral choices of each individual vary from case to case. Therefore, as the song says, "It can't be wrong, when it feels so right."

Human Nature. We share not only the same national society, we all share the same human race. As the U.S. Constitution states, all men and women have the God-given and inalienable right to life, liberty, and the pursuit of happiness—not because they were born Americans, but because they were born human beings. There is a dignity to a human being which demands that one not degrade him or her to the level of an animal or a vegetable.

Every "is" implies an "ought." If a machine is a radio, it ought to transmit sound, or it's a "bad" radio. If something is a carrot, it ought to nourish and not poison, or it's a "bad" carrot. If I am human, I ought to treat myself and all others as human, or I am a bad human. If the qualities which make human beings specifically different from animals, vegetables, or minerals are the ability to know and love, then anything which helps us all know and love is good, and anything which hinders us from knowing and loving is bad.

Role-Play

Tony Randazzo is the best hockey player on the team. It was largely because of him that Quinlan High came from a can't-win to a can't-lose squad. Not only did he practice every day till he nearly dropped, but as captain he whipped the team along till they could tell one another's moves almost telepathically. They are in the finals next week; all the college scouts will be there, not only to look at Tony but to look at other players, too. None of the players has much money, so all the seniors have their hopes pinned on Tony's "flash."

In the mid-term exams last week, Tony cheated on the chemistry exam. It wasn't a momentary whim. He and two others set up a situation to keep the teacher occupied while one of them got the exam from the teacher's desk, copied it, and returned it. The other two were Ellen Marone, Tony's girl friend, who has the lead in "My Fair Lady," and Bill Hendricks, who is in no activities but is a hockey freak.

Except for Bill, who's been caught at this several times, the other two have never been in any trouble. Their reasons this time were simple: Tony had spent all his time and energy on hockey, and he was just too busy and too tired to study. Bill offered to share his expertise. At first, Tony and Ellen were hesitant; then, they figured, who's getting hurt? They didn't pass the exam around; Ellen herself didn't even look at the exam. Tony knew that, even with the test beforehand, he wasn't likely to get better than an 80. If he flunked, he'd be ineligible to play, so he had to take the chance. If he passed, everyone would benefit, not only himself, but the other players and the school's reputation.

But they were caught. School rules require that they be suspended until the Student Court can recommend action to the principal—who need not be bound by their recommendation.

Role-Play

—Tony and his coach; Ellen and her director

—The hockey coach and the school's biggest benefactor who is also its most avid hockey fan

—Choose five judges and hold the Student Court, which will interrogate the chemistry teacher and each of the accused (who may each have a student "lawyer")

—The judges present their recommendations to the principal, even if it is a split decision.

—The principal makes the final judgment.

Notebook Question

Page 2: For yourself, put into words what you believe makes an action immoral and what elements go into forming one's conscience.

Meditation

Now a priest happened to be traveling down the same road, but when he saw the beaten man, he passed by on the other side. In the same way a Levite (deacon) who came to the place saw him, and passed by on the other side. But a Samaritan traveler who came upon him was moved with compassion when he saw him. He went up and bandaged his wounds pouring oil and wine on them; then he lifted him on to is own mount, carried him to the inn, and looked after him.

—Luke 10:31-35

The continued greed of the rich will certainly call down upon them the judgment of God and the wrath of the poor, with consequences no one can foretell. If today's flourishing civilizations remain selfishly wrapped up in themselves, they could easily place their highest values in jeopardy, sacrificing their will to be truly great to the desire to possess more. To them, we could also apply the parable of the rich man whose fields yielded abundant harvest and who did not know where to store his harvest. God said to him, "Fool, this night your soul is required of you."

—Pope Paul VI

Unit 3

Success > Truth

> "See, Biff, everybody around me is so false
> I'm constantly forced to lower my ideals."
> —*Arthur Miller*

Kent, Ohio: Within hours after four students were shot and killed by the Ohio National Guard while protesting the Vietnam War at Kent State University, several rumors spread among the local townspeople to the effect that: (1) both of the slain girls were pregnant, unmarried, and therefore obviously promiscuous;

(2) the bodies of all four were ridden with syphilis so that they would have died anyway; (3) the bodies were crawling with lice.

In fact, all four of the young people were later proven to have been clean, decent, and intelligent. In fact, two of them had not even been involved in the demonstration but were merely crossing the campus when the National Guard opened fire.

Question: Why did the local people believe as they did?

Salem, North Carolina: Jack Landry is very good at his job, in a very competitive business. In November, 1971, the company he represents had finally beaten its best competition in the tobacco industry. As a result of his efforts, Jack is now in charge of the promotion of the company's new brand of cigarettes. In a press conference to promote the new label, Landry opened his third pack of the day and told reporters that he doesn't believe all those reports about the connection between smoking and cancer or emphysema. He revealed that his company was spending ten million dollars in one year to promote the new brand.

Why a new brand? "Because it's there to be sold," Landry said. "Nearly half the adults in this country smoke. It's a basic commodity for them. I'm serving a need."

Landry is confident that the new brand will garner a 1% share of the American market in the next year. That 1% will amount to five bil-

lion cigarettes and a fine profit for Landry's company and for himself.

Question: Why does Jack Landry say and do what he does?

Dover, Delaware: At the height of the Vietnam War, a reporter visited a thriving chemical plant in this city and asked workers their feelings about their work for a chemical company which made napalm, a chemical which not only burns but adheres to the skin so that it cannot be removed without removing the skin along with it. When he showed workers in the plant (and later Air Force personnel) pictures of mothers and children, their corpses fused together by this substance, the responses were as follows: "I only deliver goods to the factory." — "I only work on the assembly line, in another department." — "I only inspect the product." — "I only off-

16

load that stuff at the shipping dock."
— "I only help load the aircraft." —
"I only make the flight plans." — "I
press a button; I do what I'm told."

The predominant feelings seem
to have been distilled in the responses of several workers and military
personnel: "I feel very sorry for
those people, but I have a family to
support."

Question: Why do the people associat-
ed with napalm answer as they do?

Pre-Test

By circling one of the numbers at the right, indicate the degree of your
agreement or disagreement with each of the following statements:
+ 2 = strongly agree; + 1 = sort of agree; − 1 = sort of disagree;
− 2 = strongly disagree.

1. The bombing of Hiroshima was justified by the
fact that, while 100,000 Japanese noncombatants
were killed, a million Japanese and Americans
would have been killed in an invasion.   + 2   + 1   − 1   − 2

2. The Jewish Sanhedrin was justified in con-
demning Jesus because, as they said, it was better
for one man to die than that the Romans should kill
the whole Jewish nation.   + 2   + 1   − 1   − 2

3. It is possible that there could be a case, sometime, when the preservation of one's reputation (even by lies, hypocrisy, or double-talk) would be more important than a single human life. $\quad$ +2 $\quad$ +1 $\quad$ -1 $\quad$ -2

4. When no student will tell a teacher who started a very serious fire (and almost all know), she is justified in punishing the whole class. $\quad$ +2 $\quad$ +1 $\quad$ -1 $\quad$ -2

5. If I lie to my mother—and she accepts it—the matter is over. $\quad$ +2 $\quad$ +1 $\quad$ -1 $\quad$ -2

6. The guards at German death camps were justified in killing Jews because, if they didn't do it, they would have been sent to the Russian front—and someone else would have killed them anyway. $\quad$ +2 $\quad$ +1 $\quad$ -1 $\quad$ -2

7. Flight personnel in military aircraft are justified in bombing areas inhabited mostly by civilians because the result will bring the enemy closer to surrender, which will be good for both sides. $\quad$ +2 $\quad$ +1 $\quad$ -1 $\quad$ -2

8. If several groups use the theater where you work as a place to trade drugs, you are justified in maintaining silence because you know that the manager is paid off, and you will lose your job and get hurt if you say anything. $\quad$ +2 $\quad$ +1 $\quad$ -1 $\quad$ -2

9. If my mother gives me too much food for my lunch at school, the only option I have is to eat it and get sick or throw it in the garbage. $\quad$ +2 $\quad$ +1 $\quad$ -1 $\quad$ -2

10. It is an entirely different matter if one cheats or cooperates in small injustices than if one cheats or cooperates in major injustices. $\quad$ +2 $\quad$ +1 $\quad$ -1 $\quad$ -2

The Maximize/Minimize Game

Divide the class into small groups, each of which will take one of the following topics and, using the personality of the persons given, brainstorm all the ways such people might maximize all the positive aspects of the case. When that begins to run down, appoint one member as a defender of the opposite side, and let the group find ways to negate or at least minimize the negative aspects of the case he or she brings up.

—Overweight people: eating.

—Tobacco executives: smoking.

—People going steady: pre-marital sex.

—Students: cheating, only on quizzes.

—San Franciscans: living on the San Andreas Fault.

—TV executives: sophomoric programming.

—German soldiers: exterminating Jews.

—South American dictators: land reform.

—Advertising executives: creating greed in children.

—TV executives: violent Saturday morning cartoons.

The Christian Gospel

Jesus said, "No servant can be the slave of two masters: he will either hate the first and love the second, or treat the first with respect and the second with scorn. You cannot be a slave both of God and of money . . . Do not say, 'What are we to eat? What are we to drink? How are we to be clothed?' It is the pagans who set their hearts on all these things." (Matthew 6:24, 31-33)

The core of the Gospel asks for a radical change in the Christian away from the values of the majority, who idolize the Economy. It asks not only for a change of one's inner life and goals, but also of one's external life-style.

(1) Do a maximize/minimize brainstorming which would enable someone to "have the best of both worlds," that is, to hold at one and the same time both the Christian values of the Gospel and the pagan values of "the World." (2) Critique each of the arguments as open-mindedly as possible.

Role-Play

Gary Snyder has been a congressman for fourteen years because he's good at it. He has brains, looks, charm, integrity, and he works hard at serving the needs of his constituents. His colleagues have put him on three very prestigious committees, one of which he chairs. When Congress is not in session, he works in a very successful law practice in the city. His family would be a credit to any man, which he honestly says is due to his wife, Ellie. The Snyders have three children: a daughter in medical school, a son just beginning law school, and a son in the seminary. Gary Snyder is a lucky man.

On November 3rd, four days before an election he was assured of winning, Gary went to a party for him at the southern tip of his district, without his wife who was home nursing a bad cold. The fatigue of campaigning was taking its toll of both of them. But the supporters at the party were old friends, and it was good to relax with them and have a few drinks. At 2 a.m. he started to drive the twenty miles home.

At 2:25, he was pulled over by a young state policeman. Gary hadn't realized that he had been going 75. What was worse, the officer smelled that he'd been drinking. He ordered Snyder to follow him back to the station for a breath test. When they got there, the captain immediately recognized the congressman and barked the young officer out of the room. The captain told Snyder he'd try to keep the whole thing out of the papers, but feared it would take some doing. He said it in a way that Gary Snyder suspected, if he gave the captain a convincing amount of untraceable cash, the papers would assuredly remain ignorant. As Snyder left for home, the captain asked him to be sure and give him a call, at home, before noon.

Role-Play
—Snyder with his wife
—Snyder with his campaign manager
—Snyder with his three children
—Snyder with his law partner
—Finally, Snyder with the captain on the phone, giving him his decision.

Notebook Question

Page 3: Unfortunately, none of us is perfect. No matter how fair and just we try to be, we always fall short, simply because we're human. Think of one injustice that is very "close to home" for you—perhaps something you yourself play The Maximize/Minimize Game with. On this page, reflect on what concrete steps you could take at least to lessen that injustice a little.

Meditation

The man and his wife heard the sound of Yahweh God walking in the garden in the cool of the day, and they hid from Yahweh God among the trees of the garden. But Yahweh God called to the man. "Where are you?" he asked.

"I heard the sound of you in the garden," the man replied. "I was afraid because I was naked, so I hid."

"Who told you that you were naked?" Yahweh God asked. "Have you been eating of the tree I forbade you to eat from?"

The man replied, "It was the woman you put me with! She gave me the fruit, and I ate it."

—Genesis 3:8-12

Therefore, those who claim their own rights, yet altogether forget or neglect to carry out their respective duties, are people who build with one hand and destroy with the other.

—Pope John XXIII

Unit 4

A Spectrum of Consciences

One may well ask, "How can you advocate
breaking some laws and obeying others?"
The answer lies in the fact that there are two
types of laws, just and unjust.
—Dr. Martin Luther King, Jr.

San Jose, California: Ed and Dorothy Ryan lived in a not-quite-middle-class section of San Jose. They'd worked all their lives, Ed as a laborer and Dorothy as a school cook. They'd married off all their five children and slowly eroded their mortgage, even managed to put some money into a small summer cottage in the hills near the Salinas Valley. Ed was ready to retire, and Dorothy was more than willing to pack in her job; the school had "gone down." So, because the house was now too big, they decided to sell it and move year-round into the cottage. With the money from the sale, they could winterize the cottage and, with their savings, live a good long life together. The land was good, and Dorothy loved to putter in the garden. Ed loved to fish.

Only one problem. All three of the families who inquired about the house were black. It was an all-white neighborhood, mostly assimilated Irish, Poles, and Italians. Dorothy was beside herself. On the one hand,

if they sold to blacks, all their old friends in the neighborhood would hate them. Property values would go down "for sure." But on the other hand, those black people could get together and kill the two of them in their beds if they didn't sell, couldn't they? "I know," she whimpered. "I've seen them at school."

Ed was calm as a clam. "Listen," he said, "did the Burkes consult us thirty years ago when they sold to them DiTuccis? C'mon, Dot, this is a business proposition. Black money's as good as white money, no?" A glint came into his eye. "And they're so eager to get out of wherever they come from, they'll pay a few thousand more than white folks, right? Listen, honey, we played by the rules. We paid our dues. Now we got a right to collect."

Denver, Colorado: Mike and Judy Falco live in a fashionable suburb of

Denver. Mike runs a very successful collision shop in the city, and Judy is, as they say, "a clubwoman." They have four children: Kim and John in college and twin boys in junior high. Kim is a high-spirited girl—and for that reason her father's pet. Her mother is a bit critical of the way Mike spoils Kim, especially with a new car for passing into senior year at Regis College. "And a car in two years for Johnny? And in five years a *pair* of cars for the twins?" But Judy's an old-fashioned, contentedly unliberated woman, so—right or wrong—Mike is boss.

Driving home from a party New Year's Eve, completely sober, Kim hit a drunken derelict on a deserted downtown street. She jammed on the brakes, jumped out of the car, and ran back. He was dead. Blind with panic, Kim ran back to her car and sped home. She blurted out the story to her parents and then, suddenly, burst into hysterics. Her mother took her upstairs, gave her a sleeping pill, and put her to bed.

As Judy came downstairs, she saw Mike staring dully at the phone. "We'll have to call the police," he said.

"Are you out of your mind?" Judy yelled. She tried to make him listen. "I'm sorry for that old man; I truly am. But what good would calling the police do? The man was a bum; nobody knew he was even alive and won't even know he's dead; he's finally out of his misery. You can get the car fixed; say it hit a tree. Mike, she's our only daughter! She's never done anyone any harm. Is she supposed to pay for the rest of her life for one mistake she wasn't even responsible for? Bad enough that she has to know it without all Denver knowing it."

"Judy, she killed a man—no matter who it was. And she left him there. She was responsible for that. They'll let her off, but she broke the law. And now we know. Do you think she'd want parents who'd condone what she did? What would happen if everybody decided for themselves whether this time was 'above the law'?"

———————————

Shreveport, Louisiana: George Ackroyd teaches chemistry, and his wife, Maggie, teaches English in the same high school. Their son, Tom, is married and a senior at Tulane. Katy, their other child, is mentally retarded and, although she lives at home on weekends, she lives and works as an aide during the week at a school for more severely handicapped children over in Malone. As an extra source of income, the Ackroyds rented out Tom's room to Cynthia Thomas, an unmarried woman who teaches French at their high school. They've become good friends, and Cynthia is happy to take care of Katy some weekends so George and Maggie can get away.

One day at school, out of the blue, rumors began to circulate that Cynthia Thomas had been fired, even though she had tenure. George was furious. Whenever he tried to find out the cause, he got nothing but "knowing" looks.

That night at home, Cynthia wept as she told them that the reason she'd been fired was that she was a homosexual. She had never, in twenty-six years of teaching, made any approach to a girl in school. She would rather have died. She'd fought it all her life, but the preceding summer vacation there had been an "episode" of a week with a woman her own age. The woman later tried to blackmail her and, when Cynthia refused to pay, she took the story to the school board.

George exploded. "By God, we're going to do something about this!" Cynthia pleaded with him; there was no way the board was going to change its ruling, and he and Beth might well lose their jobs in a futile cause. What might be worse, their friends would find the Ackroyd's "guilty by association." George Ackroyd wasn't about to be stopped by "a bunch of damn fascists." He went to the phone to see what other teachers he could enlist for a teachers' strike in protest.

Maggie was far calmer. As she held her weeping friend, she said, "Cynthia, if it means our jobs, it means our jobs. It's not just that you're a good friend. I honestly think that, even if you were a stranger, I'd try to do something about this. And even if George weren't willing to go along with me, I'd try. Maybe we won't change things, but they'll certainly know we tried. If we didn't try, I couldn't live with myself."

Pre-Test

As in the last unit, indicate the extent of your agreement or disagreement with the following positions.

A

1.	Dorothy Ryan	+2	+1	−1	−2
2.	Ed Ryan	+2	+1	−1	−2
3.	Judy Falco	+2	+1	−1	−2
4.	Mike Falco	+2	+1	−1	−2
5.	George Ackroyd	+2	+1	−1	−2
6.	Maggie Ackroyd	+2	+1	−1	−2

B

1. Dorothy Ryan should have been more careful to respect the wishes of her neighbors.	+2	+1	−1	−2
2. Ed Ryan was, justifiably, following normal business practice in jacking up prices if people paid.	+2	+1	−1	−2
3. The Ryans should have sold their home to white people.	+2	+1	−1	−2
4. Judy Falco was right in asserting that her daughter's welfare, at least in this case, dictated silence.	+2	+1	−1	−2
5. Mike Falco was therefore wrong in insisting on bringing the matter to the police.	+2	+1	−1	−2
6. In your own case, protecting your family would take precedence over even a just law.	+2	+1	−1	−2
7. George Ackroyd seems a "crusading type," too skeptical, egotistical, and self-righteous.	+2	+1	−1	−2
8. Homosexuality should automatically disqualify teachers when some or all of the students they teach are of their same sex.	+2	+1	−1	−2
9. No matter what their beliefs, once the school board had decided the case, the Ackroyd's should have minded their own business.	+2	+1	−1	−2
10. If the government held a policy you strongly opposed (abortion, nuclear proliferation, or some such), would you join a public protest, even if it would very likely land you in jail?	+2	+1	−1	−2

Consciences Grow

The following is a schematic outline of the work of Dr. Lawrence Kohlberg of Harvard University on the growth of moral insight. He saw three major *levels* in that growth as the individual widens the scope of his or her "self." These three levels are exemplified by each of the three stories at the beginning of this unit. Movement from one level to the next is really a giant step in an individual's moral growth: from selfishness, to loyalty, to principle.

At the first level, the person's concerns are limited within the confines of his or her own skin (the Ryans); at the second level, those concerns reach out to an "extended self," in which the individual will treat a limited group of persons with the same sensitivity as his or her own self (the Falcos); at the third level, concern for the other is unlimited by any artificial divisions among human beings or by any cost to the self (the Ackroyds).

Each of the levels is subdivided into two *stages,* six stages in all, according to the growth in more refined and more altruistic motivations: fear, profit, loyalty, law-and-order, the common good, and integrity.

Everyone, without exception, moves through this common pattern of growth—though many get so far and no further, no matter what their age. The stages are also invariant; it is impossible to bypass one. Finally, Kohlberg and his associates, over years of intensive study, have established that an individual at any given level cannot even *comprehend* the motivation of those two stages above himself, although he or she is susceptible to the motivations of one stage above. Thus, Judy Falco, though a woman of great love, would probably find George Ackroyd to be an incomprehensible rabble-rouser.

Level I: Pre-conventional—Comply/Compete—Self-Centered

    Stage 1: Fear (Dorothy Ryan)

        —Not law or justice, but what it will cost me.

          Conscience = self-protectiveness

          Love = Do what Mommy says; she can punish.

          God = If Mommy has clout, God has hell.

    Stage 2: Profit (Ed Ryan)

        —Minimize the pain, maximize the pleasure. But it's give-and-take, bargaining: "You scratch my back, and I'll scratch yours."

          Conscience = cunning: "Is it worth the risk?"

          Love = Do what Mommy says; it'll pay off.

          God = insurance: "How far can I go?" Or "I don't go to Mass because I don't get anything out of it."

Level II: Conventional—Cooperate/Identify—Group Centered

Stage 3: Group Loyalty (Judy Falco)

—Obligation to society, but to "one's own" first (family, gang, etc.)

Conscience = intense loyalty to my group.

Love = My Mommy, right or wrong.

God = Our God is the chief member of our group.

Stage 4: Law and Order (Mike Falco)

—Obligation to family, but over-riding obligation to laws, without which we'd have chaos.

Conscience = intense loyalty to our society's ways

Love = If Mommy sells cocaine, I turn her in.

God = The Supreme Lawgiver

Level III: Post-conventional— Internalize/Serve—Truth Centered

Stage 5: The Common Good (George Ackroyd)

—Loyalty to authority, but primarily loyalty to the truth, above any group loyalty or law.

Conscience = reason > loyalty > what others think

Love = I will not only not harm, I will rise up to defend the oppressed.

God = The One who gave us intelligence before he gave us commandments.

Stage 6: Integrity (Maggie Ackroyd)

—Would rather sacrifice any value than the integrity of one's reasoned conscience.

Conscience = personally reasoned principles about what life and human beings are for, which allow one to stand alone.

Love = I will treat every human being as I treat my own mother.

God = The One who put the truth in the natures of things and calls me to be a prophet.

Role-Play

Stan Brylski was sitting at home one Friday evening reading the paper after dinner when his wife, Edie, came in and sat down. Their only child, Karen, had just left on a date with her boyfriend, Artie Gillis.

"Well, you look serious, don't you," Stan smiled. Edie was twisting her apron in her hand. "We've got to have a talk."

"Oh? That does sound heavy. Did Karen 'borrow' your charge-card again?"

"Worse, Stan. I'm certain she's sleeping with Artie."

"Come on, Edie. I'd trust that girl anywhere, anytime, with anybody. Especially with Artie. He's a good boy, honey."

"He's a boy, Stan. And she's sixteen and pretty, and she's crazy about him, and . . ." She began to cry. Stan crossed to the couch and put his arms around her.

"Okay, honey, okay. There's something more, isn't there? She's not . . . ?"

"Oh God, not that I know. I don't think so. This afternoon, just before dinner, I picked up the phone to call mother about Sunday, and . . . and Karen was on the line talking to Artie. I started to hang up when I heard a couple of words and . . . well, I listened. Stan, there's no doubt at all."

Role-play
—Stan and Artie
—Karen and Edie
—Artie and Karen

Notebook Question

Page 4: Reflecting on all the insights and points of view you've considered in this unit, write what you, yourself, would have done in each of the problems presented in the three opening stories.

Meditation

Jesus said, "You must love the Lord your God with all your heart, with all your soul, and with all your mind. This is the greatest and first commandment. The second resembles it: You must love your neighbor as your self."

—Matthew 22:37-39

A man who does not love the brother that he can see, cannot love God, whom he has never seen.

—I John 4:20

Conscience is the most secret core and sanctuary of a human being. There he is alone with God, whose voice echoes in his depths . . . In fidelity to conscience, Christians are joined with the rest of humankind in the search for truth . . . Conscience frequently errs from invincible ignorance without losing its dignity. The same cannot be said of a person who cares but little for truth and goodness.

—Vatican II, The Church Today, 16

Unit 5

Group Selfishness

Let us not ask for possessions but for things to do.
—*Will Durant*

Newark, New Jersey: My names's Mickey Harmon. I go to this Catholic school, see, which is a royal pain in the keyster, if ya pardon my French. It's not that it's fulla nuns lashin' ya with their rosary beads or nothin' like when my old man went there. Most of them went over the wall with some priest, I think. They got a lotta faggoty men teachers that wouldn't dare come in the place except they probably got a .22 or a can o' Mace or somethin' permanent like that in their briefcase. The bad thing is they let in all these spades an' PR's 'cause the neighborhood is hittin' the skids, ya see? I mean they can't get no work down in Mississippi an' San Juan, so they come up here an' leech offa our Welfare. 'Nuff t' fry yer buns, right?

So far there ain't so many of 'em, 'cause we got tuition at this school, ya know? I mean, it's beans but it keeps out the whole armies of 'em. They mostly go to Booker T., an' spend the day carvin' up one another an' bangin' any chick-eeta they

find in a dark corner. They disgust me.

Well, anyway, most of 'em is sheep, ya know? They keep their noses clean an' spend their time tryin' t' learn English so's they can be President of the U.S. of A. I mean, can ya believe it? But there's a coupla black dudes and a handfulla PR's (with them gold teeth) that are inta knives. So we got together an' formed this society of white guys that we call "Basgetell." At first the teachers thought we was some kinda team an' we don' know howta spell, but it really means "Blacks an' Spicks Goda Hell." 'At's clever, ain't it? We got an Executive Committee of me an' four other guys, but we also got Warriors who're pretty much the football team and the wrestlers. We don't get too much crap no more from the colored element, ya know what I mean?

This society started out like a kinda protection service, ya know? But it worked so good that the Committee an' the Warriors can butt in

the head of the lunch line, even aheada the other white kids. Ya don't need no money, neither, 'cause the "studious types" is always willin' to cough up a buck to keep their glasses. Even some o' the teachers is afraid to give us detention or even flunk us. I mean, like I said, they got glasses, too, right?

Like the world belongs t' the takers, ya know? An' we're gettin' good at it. You'da done the same yerself if ya had the guts, right?

Fairbanks, Alaska: My name is Amanda Hackett. My husband, Fred, is a meteorologist connected with the U.S. Weather Service at the station here, about sixty-eight miles northwest of Fairbanks. There are eleven white families living at the station; in all, fifty-eight people—twenty-one adults and the rest are children. I teach the children in a small school. Our only other neighbors are scattered camps of Tlingit Indians. They have little to do with us except occasionally to trade at Hap Ridley's store for whiskey. In the winter, though, they come in a lot more and are pretty much dependent on the store for food; but in general they don't bother us and we don't bother them.

Last January, our men at the station became certain that in a few days we were going to be hit with a terrible snowstorm that could leave us isolated out here, completely cut off from contact with the city, for anywhere from two weeks to a month. The women got together and pretty well cleaned out Hap's store of anything edible, down to the last bean. We divided it as fairly as we could by the number of people in each family, rationing enough for each to last pretty well the full month. Hap gave us credit.

Well, the storm did come. After awhile you get used to the storms, but this one was a humdinger. After two weeks of being buried under the snow and wind, nerves get a bit frayed. Then the Indians showed up.

They'd run out of food, they said. They were starving; two children had already died. What could we do? Predictions were that the storm could blow for another two weeks. The Indians tried to force their way in through the gate, four of

them, and Fred had to fire a few shots over their heads to keep them off. They disappeared into the white blur.

Two days later the storm veered north and blew itself out. The emergency plane finally got through from Fairbanks. No one could find the Indians. Not till this spring. Their bodies, that is. There was nothing we could have done. You'd have done the same yourself.

———————

Santana, El Salvador: I am Paco Ramirez. During the planting and the harvest I work at the coffee plantation of Senor Diego Colima y Silva, for which he allows me to work a patch of his unusable land in the stony hills. It is not enough to feed us, so I leave the patch to my wife, Consuela, and the children—except for Quito who is too sickly in his chest. The others work, though, with their bloated bellies and spindly arms. And I go to the highway and try to hitch a ride to some plantation that might need a worker for a day, or to the town perhaps to weed the garden of some senora.

Today, because although I am little they feel I am a man of words, the men of the *canton* elected me to speak with Senor Colima to beg him

also to give us a small wage for the coming harvest. He is very rich, especially since the price of coffee went so high, and we can none of us spend more than one *colon* (40 cents) a day to feed our children.

"You have too many damn children," the patron yelled at me. "If you worked your field as much as you worked your wife, you'd be a rich man, Paco."

I tried to explain to him, again, that more mouths mean more to feed but more hands to make more workers. And the children die so easily. Three of my eight. But he began to shout, and I began to stammer, and I fled. I would not be the first *campesino* of Don Diego to have the electric cattle prods on my testicles.

So, sick with anger and humiliation, I took the few coins I had hoarded for my family to the *cantina* and got drunk. Perhaps this is evil in the eyes of better people, but it is better than going home to smell failure as thick in the hut as the smell from the privy, to see the children's hungry, expectant eyes fastened on their failure of a father. It was tight like a knot of barbed wire in my belly, which the *cantina* for a few moments let me forget. You would do the same.

Pre-Test

Circle True if you believe the statement is true, False if you believe it is false.

1. Thirteen conglomerates own land in the United States equal to the size of twenty-eight New Jerseys.　True　False

2. 80% of the State of Maine is owned by people who don't live in Maine.　True　False

3. The poorest 10% of American farmers get 1% of all federal subsidies, while the richest 10% get 50%.　True　False

4. Every week, 2,000 small family farms go out of business in the United States.　True　False

5. It took 300,000 years for the earth to contain two billion people; now it adds two billion every thirty years.　True　False

6. By the year 2000, there will be five billion people on planet Earth.　True　False

7. By 2000, the United States will need new housing equivalent to ten cities the size of New York City.　True　False

8. By 2000, there will be four Asians for every person considered "Western."　True　False

9. People in the United States spend three billion dollars a year on pet food and clothing for dogs and cats.　True　False

10. Every day twelve thousand people in the world die of starvation.　True　False

11. Every day ten million children are desperately hungry.　True　False

12. Today in many African countries life expectancy is one-half the life expectancy in the United States (72 years).　True　False

13. The natural resources of the world would be completely gone by the year 2000 if everyone lived as we do.　True　False

14. The United States makes up 5% of the world's population and uses 30% of the world's energy.　True　False

15. American air conditioners alone use more energy than all the people and industry in Red China.　True　False

16. One percent of Americans own 76% of all corporate stock.　True　False

17. The annual budget of New York City (8 million people) is roughly equal to the budget for all India (688 million). True False

18. In the United States 5% of the population own 60% of the land. True False

19. Each year workers work from January 1 to April 26 just to pay their taxes. True False

20. American consumers spend five billion dollars a year for cosmetics. True False

Almanac

From the section of the Almanac titled "Nations of the World," fill in the graph below:

	Pop./ mil.	GNP bil.	Per capita income	Life expectancy M	F	Doctors/ 100,000	Teachers/ 1,000
Afghanistan	_____	_____	_____	_____	_____	_____	_____
Bangladesh	_____	_____	_____	_____	_____	_____	_____
Canada	_____	_____	_____	_____	_____	_____	_____
Chad	_____	_____	_____	_____	_____	_____	_____
El Salvador	_____	_____	_____	_____	_____	_____	_____
Haiti	_____	_____	_____	_____	_____	_____	_____
India	_____	_____	_____	_____	_____	_____	_____
Laos	_____	_____	_____	_____	_____	_____	_____
USA	_____	_____	_____	_____	_____	_____	_____
Zaire	_____	_____	_____	_____	_____	_____	_____

Role-Play

Andy Vasold is a high school junior, the older of two children, the son of an accountant and a housewife. Andy is very good in school; he's never had a year-end average less than 95. He's naturally very bright and inquisitive, but he has given himself single-mindedly to learn, practically since the first grade. Silent, uncomplaining, he helps with chores around the house, but when he's finished he goes to his room and studies or pores over his stamp collection. He's seldom called to the phone except for the rare times when someone from school wants an assignment or help with a math problem. Andy's very good at math.

The problem probably began with his name. Any nitwit looking at his last name could tell what, from a very early age, his little peers were used to calling him. That was painful, but he could put up with it. What was worse was that Andy was always being praised by the teachers because he always had the right answers. He wasn't trying to show off or belittle the others, but what was he supposed to say when he was called on? Was he supposed to get 80's, just to be like everybody else? Was that why, everytime they played dodge ball in gym, right from the first grade, he was the first one to get bashed? It wasn't just because he was awkward; he was sure of that. There was something else underneath, something mean. After that, Andy was never very good at games. He began to become more interested in his reading and in his stamps.

Naturally, Andy's father is very proud of his son's academic achievements. But, again, one would have to be blind not to sense a bit of disappointment there. His father had been a second-string college basketball player. But the hoop on the Vasold's garage is rusted with disuse.

At dinner one evening, the whole family tries to get Andy to see his counselor—or anyone. But Andy looks around, helplessly. "But what's wrong? Who am I hurting?"

Role-Play
    —the family at dinner
    —Andy alone with: his father/mother; his sister/brother
    —Andy with his counselor

Notebook Question

Page 5: Congratulations! You're not going to believe this, but an eccentric millionaire has died and left you $5,000. There is, however, a catch. You can spend the money for anything you wish; you can bank part of it; but it has to be spent in five separate lots of $1,000 each. Therefore, you can't, say, use it all for college. It has to be for five different things.   (A) Choose the five ways you're going to spend the money. But be honest with yourself. This is not for a teacher; it's for your own insight.   (B) Reflecting on your choices in the light of the last five units, what do the five choices tell you about you?

Meditation

Men are "possessed" by their possessions. They think that they are worth more than others, not by what they are, but by what they own. Standing in front of his house or sitting in his car, a man can feel that he is as great as the house or the car. He tries to be more of a man than others, not by being better, but by having more property. This is one of the most common illusions of mankind. We are all more or less affected by it from childhood, even so-called good men. It is one of the grimmest obstacles to the Kingdom of God.

—The Dutch Catechism

You should carry one another's troubles and fulfill the law of Christ. It is the people who are not important who often make the mistake of thinking that they are. Let each of you examine his own conduct; if you find anything to boast about, it will at least be something of your own, not just something better than your neighbor has. Everyone has his own burden to carry.

—Galatians 6:2-5

Unit 6

Economics and Injustice—
Capitalism and Communism

There's no free lunch
—*Milton Friedman*

From each according to his ability; to each according to his needs.
—*Karl Marx*

Hutchinson, Kansas: Buell and Alice Johnson aren't ashamed that they raise hogs. It's hard work from sunup to sundown, but it's put their three kids through college. For a man and woman who never finished high school, that's not bad. People laugh at hogs, but they bring America's hog farmers between three and four billion dollars a year, and who starts his day without bacon or sausage?

Things can get too good, though. For years, hogs had brought about $63 a head, but for some reason known only to the good Lord, things have gotten out of hand the last couple of years. Either people were eating less pork, or the pigs were farrowing too heavily, but prices dropped close to $58 a head—not even enough to make expenses. The Johnsons and their friends have decided there is only one drastic way to bring prices back up—or at least get some kind of government attention. The swine breeders' association

agreed that they would all kill one-third of their herds and bury them.

A priest from a poorly funded orphanage in town came out to see the Johnsons, along with a Salvation Army major and a lady from Bread for the World, to beg them not to waste food that could sustain thousands of helpless people. At least give them away; that would have the same effect on prices.

"Look, reverends," Buell said, "I'd truly like to. But the TV people's comin' out here to film the whole thing. I'm sorry, but we gotta have some long-range protection from the federal people. And don't go lookin' at me like that. They're my pigs, and I can do what I want with 'em! It's the free enterprise system."

Providence, Rhode Island: After a six-year hitch in the Navy, Lou

Gravas had become a very well qualified machinist. So, when he settled down back home in Providence, he didn't have any wait at all to get a job with Simpson Tool and Die, a good, solid, middle-sized company. And it was just the kind of job he needed, because he had a wife and three kids, the youngest of whom, Teddy, had a blood disease which had drained away their savings.

When Lou arrived the first day on the job, Tony Caputo, the union steward, met him at his locker and, before he'd hung up his jacket, handed him the union application. Lou looked at the paper a moment and said he'd like to think about it awhile. Caputo told him it was a majority union shop, and the boss had said he'd honor that. Lou asked if that was legal. Caputo smiled and punched the locker, just hard enough, and said, "Let's say around here it's democratic. The boys'll back it up, too."

Lou had been in more than his

share of bar fights, and he wasn't impressed. "I heard this union's got ties to the Mob."

Caputo's face darkened a second, then he smiled. "Look, Gravas, you think you got a right not to join? We fight for your raises, your benefits, your pensions. We risk our jobs on a strike, so we count on strike funds. That means dues, like it or not. We risk together; we win together."

Lou grinned. "And how much does the union president make?" Caputo did not grin.

"You some kinda commie?"

"Sounds like the pot callin' the kettle black."

"You wanna work here, smart mouth, you join."

At sea, off Malaysia: Wong Kam Po, 27, had left Vietnam a month before on a small boat packed with ninety-eight people. Passage on the boat had cost each of them the equivalent of $2,000. But her father had once been a prosperous noodle merchant in the Cholon Chinese quarter of Saigon, and he had been able to pay not only the passage but fifteen taels of gold (about $5,000) more for "permission" from the new communist regime for the two of them to exile themselves.

At the harbor, the boat's human cargo had to come up with another $3,000 before the security guards would let them sail. Everything else had to be left behind—their household goods and all the stock in the store. But the alternative would have been "reassignment" to an internment camp. Since the recent Chinese invasion, the one million ethnic Chinese citizens of Vietnam, no matter how many generations they had lived there, had to leave or be imprisoned—lest they become a fifth column working within Vietnam for imperialist Peking.

Before the downfall of Saigon, Po had been estranged from her father for five years. She had been disgusted by the capitalist corruption of her get-rich-quick fellow citizens and had gone into the countryside to fight for the Viet Cong—the very people who now wanted her out of the country. Her father had searched for her, and together they had set to sea for Malaysia.

On the way, they had been stopped and boarded by Thai pirates in a rebuilt American gunboat. The marauders took what few valuables they had left and raped women at random. While a pirate held a gun on her father and forced him to watch, three of them had raped Po.

When they had reached Malaysia, after 758 miles of storms and vomiting and death, the boat was met by military police in a trawler, which began towing them back out to sea. "We can take no more!" the officer shouted from the stern of the tow boat. "We already have 75,000." After a few hours, the cable was cut, and they were left adrift.

The water rose deeper in the hull. As she stared at the heaving sea, blanketed in the smell of human feces and urine and death, Wong Kam Po—with her life behind her at 27—began to think of her once-capitalist father and her once-communist self.

Out loud, to no one in particular, she murmured, "Who won?"

Pre-Test

In the column at the right, indicate the extent of your agreement or disagreement with each of the statements which follow.

1. Buell Johnson was completely justified in destroying his hogs, since they were his own private property.

    +2   +1   −1   −2

2. Lou Gravas was obligated in justice to join Tony Caputo's union.

    +2   +1   −1   −2

3. The Vietnamese government had every right to force anyone into exile whom they considered a threat.

    +2   +1   −1   −2

4. During World War II, the United States government had every right to intern Oriental American citizens for the sake of national security. +2 +1 −1 −2

5. During that same war, there were good reasons why the government did not also intern German and Italian Americans even though we were also at war with their home countries. +2 +1 −1 −2

6. In order to make intelligent decisions in a capitalist society like the United States, every citizen should have at least a smattering of information about economics. +2 +1 −1 −2

7. Economics should be as independent of moral judgments as any other science, like physics. +2 +1 −1 −2

8. In business, efficiency and lower prices should take precedence over such old-fashioned values as sellers and consumers knowing one another. +2 +1 −1 −2

9. Communism, in all its forms, must by its very nature be both atheistic and cruel. +2 +1 −1 −2

10. The poor of South America and Africa would be better off with a fascist dictator, no matter how cruel, rather than be ruled by communists, no matter how kindly. +2 +1 −1 −2

Almanac

Fill in the most recent figures for the U.S. Industrials with the largest annual sales and, in the "Nations of the World" section, find a country with a comparable Gross Domestic Product and its population.

	Company	Sales	Country	Population
1.	_____	_____ bil.	_____	_____ mil.
2.	_____	_____ bil.	_____	_____ mil.
3.	_____	_____ bil.	_____	_____ mil.
4.	_____	_____ bil.	_____	_____ mil.
5.	_____	_____ bil.	_____	_____ mil.
6.	_____	_____ bil.	_____	_____ mil.
7.	_____	_____ bil.	_____	_____ mil.
8.	_____	_____ bil.	_____	_____ mil.
9.	_____	_____ bil.	_____	_____ mil.
10.	_____	_____ bil.	_____	_____ mil.

A Simpleton's Guide to Economics

The simpleton in question here is not the reader; it's the writer. That is to your advantage. If I knew more, I would probably blind you with theories and statistics.

There are basically three components of the economic chain: the land, the processing, and the people.

The Land

The land means farms, forests, mines, ranches, water, seed, and so on, which provide raw materials to the chain. Everything depends on resources. But the land is finite —limited; and some of its contents, like gold and oil, are nonrenewable.

But the people who depend on the land are not limited in this way. In fact, they increase every gen-eration by geometric proportion. Not only are people in a limited space going to be more and more crowded together in the future, they are going to be dividing up the resources of the land into smaller and smaller portions—or a few people are going to hog big pieces, while the rest have to have even smaller portions than if the land were divided evenly.

The Processing

In theory, the processing is quite simple: (1) getting whatever it is out of the land by farming, grazing, mining, and so forth; (2) refining the raw materials by canning, slaughtering, smelting, and so on; (3) transferring the goods along the chain and finally to a market; (4) trading or selling the final product.

41

The land is finite, but the processing can be enlarged and improved almost without limit. Compare a conglomerate's fleet of enormous harvesters with even a hundred families' hands and wagons.

The most prosperous countries are not necessarily those with plenty of space and/or rich natural resources (for example, Saudi Arabia). They can also be those who are land- and resource-poor but rich in industrious, hard-working, and shrewd people (for example, Japan, Switzerland).

Improving the processing depends only on human ingenuity—and on what society is willing to sacrifice to achieve greater efficiency, lower prices, and faster service.

At one time, a family took care of the whole economic chain, from planting to consuming, for themselves. But more efficient use of the land, faster manufacture, and wider selling (for greater profits) expanded the processing part of the chain. More capital was needed, and a whole new class of financiers and managers was born. However, as the chain stretched more and more, the human links became more and more separated, faceless, and far less concerned for one another.

The People

Originally, the people were the family, who were the owners, the workers, and the consumers. As the chain stretched out, they became divided into three separate (and often antagonistic) groups. Rights and special interest groups came more often into conflict than in the normal family.

However, the distinction between the three groups is not clear-cut: for the most part, the workers are the consumers; in some cases, the worker-consumers also own stock in a corporation and so, to some extent, are also owners. The picture is even further blurred by the fact that the old-time autocratic "Boss" has become splintered into a bewildering maze of bureaucrats and many interlocking mega-conglomerates. Ironically, these huge organizations have returned full circle to the original status: they own everything from the seed to the retail store. The only thing that has been lost is everything that "family" meant in the original system.

The owner supplies the capital, the workplace, the raw materials, and the tools. He also supplies a salary to the workers. He rightly expects to make (at least) a just profit. Sometimes he gets greedy. The workers, at every stage of the chain, add value—but also cost—to the raw materials being passed along from the source to the outlet. Rightly, they expect to be paid (at least) a just wage equal to their effort to improve the product as it passes along. Sometimes they get greedy too.

The workers, who vastly outnumber the owners, are therefore also the majority of the consumers. If they don't get enough salary from processing the products to buy the products, the owner makes no profit. If the owner pays them too much salary, he makes no profit either. Here's where most of the conflicts arise.

Today, we live in a Global Village. The economic chain that was formerly contained within the interactions of a small town is now spread like a net over the whole world. Now, very often, the president or premier of a country does not really represent his people as persons, but rather he represents his country's economy: his owners, his workers, and his consumers.

Two Economic Systems

Here we consider two extremes: the so-called "Far Right" and "Far Left." Laissez-faire capitalism (the Far Right) insists on all power to the owners; communism (the Far Left) insists on all power to the workers. Ironically, they are founded on the same basis: the sole purpose of society is to create and consume goods. They are, in these extreme positions, completely disinterested in human beings except insofar as they are *economic* factors—just as a physicist might consider a girl only as a moving object, and a sociologist might consider her only as a potential breeder.

The extreme capitalist fears that sentimentality will make government bow to workers (who both vote and cause ruckuses) and gradually eat away his individual right to increase profits.

The extreme communist fears that greed will make government bow to owners (who both contribute to campaign funds and hire lobbyists) and gradually eat way the workers' right to eat.

American democracy, which we will consider in the next unit, tries to resolve this collision of rights by steering like a cautious driver, correcting first to the right, then to the left.

Capitalism

The great and chief end of men's uniting into commonwealths and putting themselves under government is the preservation of their property.

—*John Locke*

At its most extreme, capitalism deifies competition and is willing to sacrifice all other elements to the *process*. It relies heavily on enlightened self-interest. It is like any form of athletic competition: you learn the rules, work hard, feel out your opponents' weaknesses and capitalize on them. Every American child begins to learn what capitalism means the first day he or she plays Monopoly.

Extreme capitalists would be happiest if the State and the Economy were completely separate operations, just as they would prefer the Church and the Economy to be completely separate operations. Nevertheless, there are some functions which no company, however huge, can do to protect its own operations: defend against foreign attack, preserve law and order, furnish some services that would not be profitable for private enterprise (roads, harbors, schools, mental hospitals). Thus, the State is necessary, as are taxes, as long as their intrusions are minimal.

Barring that, the State should not intrude on business: by factory inspections, wage and hour laws, child labor laws, unemployment insurance, racial and sexual quotas, and pure food and drug laws. Above all, it should not take money from hardworking people, and give it to laggards in the form of welfare. Companies will police their own yards, and voluntary charity is infinitely preferable to government doles which penalize the thrifty and reward the indolent. The basic law of capitalism is the survival of the fittest.

According to a laissez-faire capitalist, the purchase of Manhattan Island for $24 worth of beads was Stage 6 thinking; according to Lawrence Kohlberg, it was Stage 2 morality.

But capitalism has many distinct advantages. It puts economic decisions into the hands of men and women who know what they're doing. It is far more efficient than every man or woman for themselves, obstructing progress with endless bickering, getting in one another's way. It can deal with big challenges in a big way. Conglomerates can afford to buy in huge quantities, at a cheaper price, and therefore with a lower mark-up to the customer. That very efficiency and bigness is good for everybody:more goods, with uniform quality, at cheaper prices. The more the owner's profits, the higher the workers' salaries, and the more tax money, generated from both owners and workers, for roads, parks, research, and so forth. The two things laissez-faire capitalism can't cope with are a difference in talent and luck, on the one hand, and natural animal selfishness on the other.

Communism

The faithful all lived together and owned everything in common; they sold their goods and possessions and shared out the proceeds among themselves according to what each one needed.

—*Acts 2:44-45*

Roughly speaking, for the extreme capitalist, the individual's success is more important than the common good; for the communist, the common success is more important than the individual good. While laissez-faire capitalism hopes for the complete separation of the State and the Economy, communism hopes for the complete fusion of the State and the Economy.

The game of Monopoly begins as a communism: everybody has the same amount of money. But sooner or later it becomes a capitalism, with the money and property gradually in fewer and fewer hands. Economic history was the same way. In the beginning, there was more than plenty for everybody, but gradually conquest and merger turned it into a capitalism. This is what communism was born to change.

Communism needn't be atheistic or cruel. The early church was a communism: the early Christians pooled all their wealth and drew from it only what they needed. The rest was available for any other community member in need. Even today, men and women in religious orders and congregations still do the same, by vow. But in both cases it was a way of life freely chosen, not imposed by a small group in power or by conquest as heartless as any capitalist conquest. What's more, it respects not only the collectivity but every individual in the collectivity. Neither can be said of the national communisms we know today.

Karl Marx was an economist and as interested in Gross National Products as any capitalist economist, since the GNP is the index of our improvement as a State. But it was his belief that, since it was the worker who gave the marketable value to raw goods, all profit should go (ultimately) to the worker. Marx predicted (in some places, quite correctly) that the gap between the rich and poor would widen so drastically that finally, out of the workers' frustration, the explosive revolution would come. Ghetto riots and Central American revolutions are evidence enough of that. Both Marx and Lenin made no effort to deny the inevitable conflict. In fact, their agents are specifically trained to foment that conflict.

Marxism (at least in theory) also has its advantages. It deals with the poor multitudes, who by far outnumber the rich. It offers a future goal of justice, for all. It gives a plan for action, now. But the two things Marxism cannot cope with are a difference in talent and luck, on the one hand, and natural animal selfishness on the other. Just like capitalism.

Role-Play

It is the day of the great Meeting of the New Embryos. The area is quiet, dim, undifferentiated. There is a strange, otherworldly music playing somewhere in the background. The group of embryos, preparing to be sent in the next dispatch to Earth, sits to discuss the "Rules of the Game"—so that every one of them will continue to have the same equal chance they have at this moment.

You have as yet no idea in the embryonic state what each of you is to be born as: male/female, black/red/yellow/white, shy/self-confident, loved/tolerated/abused; strong/sickly/crippled, and so on.

Brainstorm the most basic laws you want to find when you arrive that will give everybody the same chances. Remember, sheer self-interest dictates that safeguards be made for the weakest, since *you* may be one of the weakest. On the one hand, avoid the unrealizeably vague ("Everybody's got to be nice to everybody else.") On the other hand, you can't foresee every single case ("Subsidies should be given to black female blind dressmakers.")

Notebook Question

Page 6: You're the chief executive officer of an enormous canning factory which also owns its own immense farms. You pay the workers in your fields the minimum wage, which is more than many of your competitors do. But you discover that if you relocate your farm operation to Mexico, you can get Mexican workers for nearly two dollars an hour cheaper than American workers. You can also make a reasonable profit selling the land.   (A) Draw a line down the center of the notebook page and list all the advantages and disadvantages, both financial and moral, of each of the two choices: relocating and staying here.   (B) In a sentence, state which choice you yourself would make.

Meditation

You should be ashamed. Is there really not one reliable man among you to settle differences between brothers, and so one brother brings a court case against another in front of unbelievers? It is bad enough for you to have lawsuits against one another at all. Oughtn't you to let yourselves be wronged, and let yourselves be cheated? But you are doing the wronging and cheating, and to your own brothers.

—I Corinthians 6:6-8

It is shameful and inhuman to use human beings as things for gain and to put no more value on them than what they are worth in muscle and energy.

—Pope Leo XIII

Unit 7

American Ideal/American Dream

"I tell ya, it's just plain goddam *democratic*
when the best man wins!"
—*Paul Hemphill*

Las Vegas, Nevada: Nicky Chase (born: Nikolas Chester Ylvisacker) is a hustler, and always has been. He grew up—like so many of his show-business heroes—on the lower East Side of Manhattan. With a name like his, Nicky learned quickly how to hold his own in a fight. He began as a shoeshine boy, working Times Square, keeping his eyes peeled. Three times a day, he "found himself" sitting across the street from the local precinct at shift changes; so Nicky knew every plainclothes cop in the area. Whenever a plant was sauntering along 42nd St., trying to look like a conventioneer from Dubuque, Nicky passed the word to the hookers. At first it was because he felt sorry for them, anybody who had to earn a living that way. Then, their grateful pimps began slipping him a twenty, maybe even a fifty for a good day. When he was fourteen, Nicky Chase was making ten or eleven grand a year from that and various other enterprises.

It was about that time that Ray Wallace of the *Daily News* spotted this ferret-faced kid and began slipping him a few bucks for human interest stories about Times Square. It was through Ray that Nicky went to his first fight at Madison Square Garden and got the idea of managing a few kids from the old neighborhood. It paid off—not with money the way the streets had, but with people—important people. Nicky was a charmer, and before long he was booking acts into the Catskills and working as an agent for young kids just starting out in show business.

Then, one of his singers, Toni Morgan, went off like a skyrocket. And Nicky had 10% of the fireworks! Broadway, Hollywood, Vegas!

Nicky now owns 51% of the Gold Flamingo, and that's only for starters. There are big movie deals, too. As he sat having a drink between shows with his old pals, Pancho and Ricky and Gabe, Nicky said something profound: "Only in America," he sighed. "You know, guys? We *are* The American Dream."

Tallahassee, Florida: Barry Gardner was a junior at McGruder College, majoring in political science. His family were smalltime farmers, but Barry had brains and he worked hard. After his first year, the college awarded him the Harlan Meade Scholarship for the freshman who showed the most promise in political science or government affairs. The prize was given in the name of a wealthy citrus grower, an alumnus of the college, who had also served a term as Deputy Undersecretary of Agriculture. It was a hefty award: $15,000.

Barry's roommate, Al Gordon, was also a poli-sci major and somewhat of a firebrand. Barry kept telling him that, if he spent more time on the books and less time painting placards, he might graduate. But Al's current crusade caused Barry something much stronger than bemusement. Al had discovered that none other than Harlan Meade, "statesman, philanthropist, and slave-owner," was paying migrants twenty-five cents a bushel to pick his oranges.

"Barry, you gotta *see* them out there! They got little kids with snot all over their noses, pullin' down those things till their arms go stiff. We're gonna picket outside old man Meade's office downtown. Maybe the papers and the TV'll pick it up. You comin'?"

Barry was angry. "Will you use your head for once, Al! That guy's my bread and butter. You're not risking fifteen grand, pal. You're just playing little liberal games."

"Listen, *pal*, the only reason you've *got* your fifteen grand is because that old skinflint pays peons dirt! Then he can play the big liege lord and educate the undeserving poor."

"Get outta here, Al," Barry growled. Al went to the door and turned. "While I'm gone, write a learned paper about 'The American Way,' Bare. Maybe you'll get a Guggenheim Fellowship!" And he slammed out.

Stockholm, Sweden: Friends with whom he'd studied at Oxford considered Bjorn Thorvaldsen the luckiest man in the world to be living where he was. Sweden is a socialist "welfare state," but nothing like Merrie England. Taxes are enormously high; so there is little incentive to amass great wealth. But there is no real defense expenditure to draw government attention away from the people. The total population is about the size of New York City, inhabiting a country as big as California. There are no slums; poverty has almost ceased to exist; unemployment is below 2%; and per capita income is the highest in the world.

Moreover, hospitals are free; both father and mother may take off for three months at the birth of a child, at 90% pay. A child allowance is paid for each child under sixteen; there are numerous day-care centers; and university students receive generous study allowances, loans, and grants. Every worker is guaranteed four weeks vacation. Unlike communist countries, the state does not dictate jobs. Instead it offers "removal grants" to encourage families to move where work is available— another reason for the lack of slums. And 90% of industry is still privately owned.

Nonetheless, last Friday evening after work, Bjorn told his wife that he wanted to go alone up to their cabin in the mountains. He had a lot to think over. For several hours he sat in the warm cabin, surrounded by icy quiet outside, staring into the fire.

Then, at 1:28 a.m., Bjorn Thorvaldsen rose from his chair, took his revolver into the cold white night, and put a bullet into his brain.

Oddly, Sweden also has the highest suicide rate in the world.

Pre-Test

Indicate the extent of your agreement or disagreement with each of the statements that follow.

1. The United States Government should provide free child day-care for welfare mothers who want to work and get their families off public assistance.	+ 2	+ 1	− 1	− 2
2. Every American has a right to a college education, even if he or she can't pay for it.	+ 2	+ 1	− 1	− 2
3. Every American has a right to the same quality of education, even if it means bussing to obtain racial and educational balance in our schools.	+ 2	+ 1	− 1	− 2

4. Every American, regardless of race, has a right to buy a home for sale in your neighborhood if he or she has the money to pay for it.	+ 2	+ 1	− 1	− 2
5. The United States has an enormously disproportionate share of the world's wealth, which is objectively unjust.	+ 2	+ 1	− 1	− 2
6. "If you have two coats, and your brother has none, give your brother one of your coats."	+ 2	+ 1	− 1	− 2
7. In America, a family does not have any right to goods or services or money which they have not worked for.	+ 2	+ 1	− 1	− 2
8. American society is unjust unless some way is found to see that every American, no matter who, has at least enough food to keep from starving.	+ 2	+ 1	− 1	− 2
9. Provided most cheaters can be eliminated, the helpless must be fed and sheltered, even if it means my taxes are raised and I have to live less well.	+ 2	+ 1	− 1	− 2
10. Even if the worthwhile land in a particular area is limited, anyone is justified in buying up as much of it as he or she can pay for.	+ 2	+ 1	− 1	− 2

Almanac

A

Before you look up the answers to the following questions in the Almanac, make a quick run through and guess, jotting your guesses in pencil.

1. What is the largest source of income tax revenue for the United States Treasury?

1._____

2. From what income bracket does the government get the most money in individual income taxes?

2._____

3. In terms of 1967 dollars, what is the purchasing power of a dollar today?

3._____

4. (A) What is the average size farm in the United States?

4.(A)_____

(B) What is the average size farm in Arizona?

(B)_____

(C) What is the average annual farm income in the United States?

(C)_____

5. What is the poverty level in terms of annual salary for a family of:

Four	Five	Six	Seven	Eight
_____	_____	_____	_____	_____

6. (A) How many Americans are officially "poor"? 6.(A)_____

    (B) How many are white? (B)_____

    (C) How many are black? (C)_____

7. How much does a person on unemployment make a week in:

    (A) Michigan 7.(A)_____

    (B) New York (B)_____

    (C) Mississippi (C)_____

8. If a family spends more than a quarter of its weekly budget on food, how much can an unemployment family of four spend per person each day on food in those three states?

    (A) Michigan 8.(A)_____

    (B) New York (B)_____

    (C) Mississippi (C)_____

9. What is the current price for one Big Mac or one Whopper or similar burger? 9._____

10. What is the average amount in purchasing power of welfare per week for:

    (A) old people 10.(A)_____

    (B) parents of dependeant children (AFDC) (B)_____

    (C) the blind (C)_____

    (D) the disabled? (D)_____

B

"Adjusted Gross Income" means the amount of a person's salary that is subject to payroll taxes (Federal withholding, FICA, and State withholding) after the legally allowable nontaxed deductions are granted for (4) dependents. E.g., gross of $11,300 minus adjustment for four dependents, $4,000, equals $7,300 adjusted gross, minus FICA and withholding taxes, equals net pay. Below are five adjusted gross incomes. Find in the Almanac the average Individual Income Tax Returns for each group's bracket, calculate the percentage of income going for taxes, and the money left over. Then, if a family of four were to spend about one-fourth of its income on food (usually more), find out how much each family could spend on food per person each day: therefore, what's left after taxes divided by four (amount for food), divided by 365 (days), divided again by four (family members).

Adj. Gross Income	Av. Tax	%	Left	Food
$7,300 (min. wage)	_____	_____	_____	_____
$9,900 (pov. lvl)	_____	_____	_____	_____
$24,000	_____	_____	_____	_____
$96,000	_____	_____	_____	_____
$998,000	_____	_____	_____	_____

C

Political Action Committees (PAC's) contribute to political campaigns in the names of corporations, unions, and so forth. Who were the top five contributors, and what sums did they contribute?

1._____

2._____

3._____

4._____

5._____

Bonus: Can you guess the source of the following quotation:

> Whenever any form of government becomes destructive of these ends, it is the right of the people to alter or to abolish it, and to institute new government, laying its foundation on such principles and organizing its power in such form as, to them, it shall seem most likely to effect their safety and happiness. It is their right, it is their duty, to throw off such government and to provide new guards for their future security.

_____

America: Competition and Cooperation

Condensed expressions of the two extreme positions with regard to the functions of government which we studied in the last unit were proposed by Alexander Hamilton (The Right) and Thomas Jefferson (The Left).

Hamilton believed that freedom is the general rule, and restraint should be the exception. There should be no constraint on free enterprise and no limits on the opportunity for anyone to acquire goods and land. (Abraham Lincoln later voiced the same opinion: government should do for the people only what the people *cannot* do for themselves.)

Jefferson argued to the contrary that private property is a relative value, not an absolute value. The government's responsibility is not merely to prevent injury to rights (double negative) but also to guarantee a fair distribution of American resources (positive). In fact, a passage (later rejected) in the original draft of the Constitution stated: "An enormous proportion of property vested in a few individuals is dangerous to the right and destructive to the common happiness of mankind; and therefore, every free state hath the right to discourage possession of such property."

Along with Benjamin Franklin, Jefferson believed that no one ought to own more property than he needed for a living. The rest belonged to the State, that is, to everyone in common. Jefferson surely saw the need for *some* property as a guarantee of the individual's freedom, but property was also seen as a danger, once it created dramatic inequality between individual Americans.

Classical Forms of Justice

These two conflicting theories on the role of government are reflected in the three classical areas of justice: commutative justice, distributive justice, and social justice.

Commutative Justice (Latin, *commutare*, to exchange back and forth) is rooted in the right to private property, as Alexander Hamilton argued. It deals with claims between individuals and groups when different rights come into conflict. It insures that the boss gives you your check at the end of the week, that Mobil Oil won't plant an oil rig on your front lawn uninvited, and that nobody can play your song without paying you for it.

Distributive Justice (Latin, *distribuere*, to spread around) is rooted in the individual's right to life which includes having enough food, clothing, and shelter to keep him or her from starving or dying of exposure. It says nothing of the quality of the food, clothes, and shelter; it speaks only of *sufficiency*. Thomas Jefferson argued that all human beings have these rights consistent with their human dignity (which no Pekinese or Porsche has). This right exists even in those whose contribution to the economic process is minimal or non-existent: children, the aged, the handicapped. Even the town drunk.

Social Justice is called into play when the claims of distributive justice (a share of the essentials) come into conflict with the claims of commutative justice (private property). We saw social justice come into play in the cases of Sister Therese's school locks, ice cream, and fire extinguishers, the contents of Hap Ridley's store, Buell Johnson's hogs, and many others.

Role-Play

Corlene Jefferson worked as a nurse's aide at County Hospital. She began as a woman in her 50s, but it was a job she was born to do. She had endless patience and kindness for the sick, and her quick black hands were both deft and soothing. She was more than willing to cover for any aide who was sick, often doing two shifts—and the work of two women on each. What's more she had the instincts of a good diagnostician, even outguessing the young interns at times. She'd chuckle and say, "I guess one of my great-granddaddies must have been a witch doctor!"

So skilled was she that the overworked nurses on Third South often asked Corley to give injections—even though it was strictly forbidden. She was better at it than many of them. For that reason, the nurses were always trying to get her to go to school, to become at least a licensed practical nurse. She had the skills, and it would mean more money. But Corley kept saying that she was too old for that and, besides, she needed the money now, not down the road. Everyone knew Corley's husband, Harry, was "home ill" and, because of her job—and her pride—neither of them would ask for public assistance.

Earlier this month, the chief administrator hired a management firm to investigate the whole hospital to see if there were ways to cut skyrocketing costs—not only to the patients but to the hospital itself. Nobody liked the intrusion of "the young snoops" in their already too-demanding work. But one of the investigators found evidence that, over the course of six years, small amounts of expensive antibiotics had disappeared unaccounted for from the drug supply room. Overall, it was worth several thousand dollars. Then he discovered, beyond doubt, that the thief had been Corlene Jefferson.

In the chief administrator's office, she wept and confessed that her husband was dying of cystic fibrosis. The antibiotics he needed were so expensive that she couldn't possibly afford to buy them. That was why she had worked so much harder than the other aides, without pay, to "make it up."

It was the recommendation of the management firm that Corlene Jefferson either repay the cost of the antibiotics or be prosecuted.

Role-Play
    —The chief administrator, the head nurse, and the young investigator
    —Corley and the head nurse
    —A jury of twelve debating the case and giving a verdict.

Notebook Question

Page 7:   Reflect on the positions of "The Left" and "The Right" on the question of public assistance, such as welfare.   (A) To which side do you "lean"; to which one more than the other?   (B) Try to explain the reasons for your position.

Meditation

Land must not be sold in perpetuity, for the land belongs to Me, and to Me you are only strangers and guests.

—Leviticus 25:23

It is a monstrous masterpiece of this age to have transformed man, as it were, into a giant as regards the order of nature, yet in the order of the supernatural and eternal, to have changed him into a pygmy.

—Pope Pius XII

If a person is in extreme necessity, he has the right to take from the riches of others what he himself needs.

—Vatican II, The Church Today

Unit 8

Christianity and Injustice

Isn't it a shame that the impious Galileans
support not only their own poor in the typhus epidemic
but also ours—while we neglect altogether
to make provision for them?

—*Julian the Apostate*

Buffalo, New York: My Dad was what used to be called a "jobber." He and my uncle, Dan Murphy, bought food items in bulk from wholesalers and then sold them in smaller lots to family-owned grocery stores. Dan worked in the office, supervised the warehouse and the five drivers, and Dad drove another truck, supervised the routes, and drummed up business. It wasn't a big business, but it was comfortable.

When Uncle Dan died, Dad took on a partner named Tom Miles. Now my mother—who could read a man the way a gypsy reads tea leaves—kept insisting that Tom Miles was, in his best moments, a crook, and that he was going to fleece Dad for every nickel he had. But my Dad—who was the gentlest man I ever knew—kept answering, "Now, Bea, you're too darn suspicious."

Well, late one Sunday morning, my Dad got word that Tom Miles, his wife, and two little daughters had skipped town with a truckload of merchandise—and the entire business bank account. Young as I was, I'll never forget that Sunday. And it got worse.

My Dad refused to prosecute.

Was he insane? It wasn't just the bank account; what about all the outstanding bills? "Look," he said to the family, "I trust the three of you. We can make it. We'll all have to work very hard, but we'll pay back every penny, and we'll come out okay."

All the things the boys in my high school had, I never had. I wore the same suitcoat to school for three years. We never went on vacation. I worked from the time I was twelve, after school and summers. Mom and Dad worked six days a week. Why? What was Dad's reason?

"I don't want those two little girls growing up knowing their father is a convict."

———————

Salem, Oregon: Sister Catherine hadn't had a cigarette in seventeen years; but as she sat in the finally-empty auditorium, she let out a sigh and said, "What I wouldn't give for a smoke right now!" She had just heard 286 girls, over the course of four afternoons, one after another, sing "I'm Gonna Wash that Man Right Outta My Hair" as a tryout for *South Pacific.* If they'd been within reach, Kit would have cheerfully choked Richard Rodgers, Oscar Hammerstein, III, *and* Mary Martin. But it was over. All except the cuts—down to forty-eight girls, unless they were going to put the show on at the State Fairgrounds!

That night, sitting in her room, she made the cuts. There were nine or ten obviously fine voices, possible leads, about forty who couldn't carry a tune in a washtub, and 156 who ranged from "Weeelll ..." to "Ho-hum." With the dogged patience of an admissions officer at Harvard, she balanced all the factors: poise, movement, size, vocal range. And, yes, need. Some girls were so lonely and had mustered such courage that . . . well, she always padded out the last five with "homelies," even if there were girls with slightly better voices.

Next day she posted the final cuts. Some girls shrieked with joy and swooned decorously; some looked stilettos right into Sister Kit's heart. And before morning recess, she had a call from Mr. Ernest Bloch. Mr. Ernest Bloch was the biggest benefactor of the school. Mr. Ernest Bloch's daughter, Gretchen, had not made the show.

"Now, Sister," his voice exuded good fellowship, "couldn't you just open up just the tiniest little space for Gretchen in the back of the chorus?"

"Mr. Bloch, I cut 166 girls. If I opened up just the tiniest little space for each of them, I'd have to put the chorus in the seats and the audience on the stage. In fairness . . . ."

"But, Sister," a bit more of an edge in the voice now, a bit more of the businessman, "I really didn't mean to bring up past generosities, but . . . ."

"Mr. Bloch, there are girls whose fathers haven't the money to insure their daughters a part." Maybe, she thought, I could cut one "homely"?

"Thank you for your time, Sister. I'll just have a talk with the principal. Goodbye."

Oh, God, she thought, what I wouldn't give for a smoke right now.

———

Phoenix, Arizona: Philip Lawrence was a very wealthy man indeed. He had begun as a young architect with a small building firm and slowly developed a broad base of trust around the city, not only for his talent but for his good business judgment. Taking the risk at thirty-two, with good capital support from the friends he'd cultivated, he'd moved out on his own. Now, at fifty-two, he had six different developments around Phoenix, and he would never have to work another day in his life. But Phil couldn't stay away from the office. It had become his whole life. Any hour away was just "treading water" till he could get back to what he truly loved.

Phil's boys were a disappointment. One after another they had married "beneath" them—a cocktail waitress from Vegas, a mousy grade-school teacher, and a bleachy beautician. Oh, his wife, Sharon, invited them over at the proper times,

trying to patch things up, and Phil tolerated that. But the last child, Debbie—she was the one! She had good sense, that girl. As soon as she graduated from high school, Debbie was coming into the business; learn right from the bottom up.

Then, in January of her senior year, Debbie got pregnant. When he heard, Phil struck her across the face with his open hand and stormed out of the house. Two days later he came home, sobered, and sat down with his wife in their den.

"If the bum that did it will do the right thing, I'll give her the same kind of wedding the boys had. I'll give her away, and I'll be at the reception." He paused. "I'll give her justice."

Sharon bit back the tears, angrily. "Good God, Phil, she could get justice from a judge!"

"I'm giving her all a man could be asked to give! What more can I give her?"

"Love!" Sharon cried. "And forgiveness!"

And she left her husband, alone.

Pre-Test

1. In the first story, my Dad was   (A) a fool in the eyes of the world;   (B) lousy at being a capitalist;   (C) a Christian;   (D) all of these.

2. Sister Kit should have   (A) done just what she did;   (B) added Gretchen, for the good of the school;   (C) left the decision up to the principal;   (D) offered Gretchen a minor lead.

3. At least in this case, according to the Kohlberg scale, Phil Lawrence was: (A) Stage 2;   (B) Stage 3;   (C) Stage 4;   (D) Stage 5.

4. Faith is   (A) a blind leap without evidence;   (B) an assent made only after every bit of evidence is weighed;   (C) the result of both calculation and risk;   (D) an assent made under threat of eternal punishment.

5. The greatest obstacle to faith is: (A) rational skepticism;   (B) fear of the cost;   (C) selfishness;   (D) unwillingness to think for oneself.

6. Which of the following was *not* a characteristic of Yahweh in the eyes of the Hebrews: (A) the rescuer of the oppressed, whether Jew or Gentile;   (B) the faithful bridegroom of the often whorish Israel;   (C) the vengeful destroyer of all who sin;   (D) the only true King of Israel.

7. The Christian social program embodied in the Sermon on the Mount is a call to: (A) competition to see who can be most holy;   (B) cooperation with other religions;   (C) total reversal of capitalist values;   (D) complete material poverty for all.

8. According to Jesus, the only norm for one's rejection from Heaven will be: (A) sins of cruelty and sexuality;   (B) ignoring the needy;   (C) failure to worship and pray;   (D) refusal of Christian baptism.

9. According to Jesus, anyone who is rich: (A) is the privileged servant of the poor;   (B) is successful because God has rewarded his industry;   (C) should be ashamed that he is wealthy while so many starve;   (D) should give away all he has and become poor himself.

10. According to Jesus, the poor are: (A) lucky because they have so little to worry about losing;   (B) holy because of their state and incapable of real sin;   (C) encouraged to accept their suffering as a blessing from God;   (D) beloved of Yahweh, who is always biased in favor of the needy.

Heroes

In the spaces below, list in order the men and women you consider heroes, people who—no matter what their field—give a good example and a good feeling to you and to the youth of America. (Better write in pencil in case you change your ordering.)

1._____   6._____

2._____   7._____

3._____   8._____

4._____   9._____

5._____   10._____

Almanac

1.   In terms of salary alone, the President of the United States makes $200,000 a year. How many professional athletes make ten times his salary?

1._____

2.   How many make five times his salary?

2._____

3.   Of the eighty-six top-paid professional athletes listed by the Almanac, how many make more than the President of the United States?

3._____

4.   Who is the highest paid governor?

4._____

5.   What is the salary of a cabinet member?

5._____

6.   What is the salary of the Chief Justice?

6._____

7.   What is the salary of a United States Senator?

7._____

8.   What is the salary of a U.S. Representative?

8._____

9. In the most recent survey, who are the top three heroes of American youth, male and female, and what two things do they have in common?

9._____

_____

_____

10. Yes/No: Would you ever personally consider a career in public life? (elected office, etc.)

10._____

Justice and the God of the Hebrews

Woe to the legislators of infamous laws,
to those who issue tyrannical decrees,
who refuse justice to the unfortunate
and cheat the poor among my people of their rights,
and who make widows their prey
and rob the orphan.
What will you do on the day of punishment,
when, from far off, destruction comes?
—*Isaiah 10:1-3*

Yahweh, who does what is right,
is always on the side of the oppressed.
—*Psalm 103:6*

Yahweh, forever faithful,
gives justice to those denied it,
gives food to the hungry, gives liberty to prisoners.
—*Psalm 146:7*

I know Yahweh will avenge the wretched,
and see justice done for the poor.

—*Psalm 140:12*

I have made my decree and will not relent:
because they have sold the virtuous man for silver
and the poor man for a pair of sandals,
because they trample the heads of ordinary people
and push the poor out of their path.

—*Amos 2:6-7*

You must not molest the stranger or oppress him, for *you* lived as strangers in the land of Egypt. You must not be harsh with the widow or with the orphan; if you are harsh with them, they will surely cry out to me, and be sure I shall hear their cry. My anger will flare and I shall kill you with the sword; your wives will be widows, and your children will be orphans.

—*Exodus 22:20-24*

Break unjust fetters and undo the thongs of the yoke, to let the oppressed go free and break every yoke, to share your bread with the hungry, to shelter the homeless poor, to clothe the man you see to be naked.

—*Isaiah 58:6-7*

[Job, the perfect and upright Hebrew said:] Who but I was father of the poor? Have I ever seen a wretch in need of clothing, or a beggar going naked, without his having cause to bless me from his heart as he felt the warmth of the fleece from my lambs?

—*Job 26:16, 31:18-19*

Begins to sound like a pattern, doesn't it?

Justice and the God of Jesus Christ

The Magnificat

He has pulled down princes from their thrones and exalted the lowly. The hungry he has filled with good things, and the rich he has sent, empty, away.

—Luke 1:52-53

The Inaugural Address

The spirit of the Lord has been given to me, for he has anointed me. He has sent me to bring the good news to the poor, to proclaim liberty to captives and to the blind new sight, to set the downtrodden free, to proclaim the Lord's year of favor.

—Luke 4:16-30

The Sermon on the Mount

You have heard how it was said: You must love your neighbor and hate your enemy. But I say this to you: love your enemies and pray for those who persecute you; in this way you will be sons of your Father in heaven.

—Matthew 5:43-45

Do not store up treasures for yourselves on earth, where moths and woodworms destroy them and thieves can break in and steal. But store up treasures for yourselves in heaven, where neither moth nor woodworms destroy them and thieves cannot break in and steal. For where your treasure is, there will be your heart also.

—Matthew 6:19-21

Why worry about clothing? Think of the flowers in the fields; they never have to work or spin; yet I assure you not even Solomon in all his regalia was robed like one of these.

—Matthew 6:28

The Judgment

Next he will say to those on his left hand, 'Go away from me, with your curse upon you, to the eternal fire prepared for the devil and his angels. For I was hungry and you never gave me food; I was thirsty and you never gave me anything to drink; I was a stranger and you never made me welcome, naked and you never clothed me, sick and in prison and you never visited me.'

Then it will be their turn to ask, 'Lord, when did we see you hungry or thirsty, a stranger or naked, sick or in prison, and did not come to your help?'

Then he will answer, 'I tell you solemnly, in so far as you neglected to do this to one of the least of these, you neglected to do it to me.'

—*Matthew 25:41-46*

Begins to look like a pattern, doesn't it?

The Statue of Liberty

Not like the brazen giant of Greek fame,
With conquering limbs astride from land to land:
Here at our sea-washed, sunset gates shall stand
A mighty woman with a torch, whose flame
Is the imprisoned lightning, and her name:
Mother of Exiles. From her beacon-hand
Glows world-wide welcome; her mild eyes command
The air-bridged harbor that twin cities frame.
"Keep, ancient lands, your storied pomp!" cries she
With silent lips. "Give me your tired, your poor,
Your huddled masses yearning to breathe free,
The wretched refuse of your teeming shore.
Send these, the homeless, tempest-tost to me.
I lift my lamp beside the golden door!"

Emma Lazarus

Begins to look like a pattern, doesn't it?

Role-Play

Bishop Patrick Hingley had an embarrassingly sudden conversion when he was sixty-three years old. It really surprised him. He had been a very good bishop for ten years. The diocese was out of debt; he'd built two new high schools; he sat on the boards of a college, a bank, and the United Way. He assigned priests shrewdly and listened patiently to their complaints. He had steered his people through the rocky aftermath of Vatican II.

Then to celebrate his thirty-fifth anniversary as a priest and his eighteenth as bishop, the people of his diocese—non-Catholic and Catholic alike—had raised the money to give him a three-month trip around the world. It had been wonderful! The theaters in Dublin and London, the restaurants in Paris, the shrines at Lourdes, Rome, and the Holy Land.

And then he made his big mistake. He stopped off for two days to visit the convent of Mother Teresa of Calcutta before his final month in Hong Kong, Taiwan, Japan, and Hawaii. He watched the orphanage nuns bring in babies they'd found in garbage cans. He visited the leper hospitals and saw hundreds of human beings literally rotting to death—but loved. One morning he walked the silent streets with a Belgian priest, lifting the dying derelicts from gutters into a wooden cart.

He stayed a month.

When he returned, he sold his Chrysler and bought a Volkswagen. He sold his gold crozier, cross, and ring, and got wooden ones. He sold the bishop's house and moved into a ghetto parish. He gave the money to the diocesan Catholic Charities.

His brother, Howard, a lawyer, thought Pat had caught some Eastern disease. The men in his country club said they weren't giving any more to diocesan drives because they doubted the bishop was capable of handling money anymore. Howard's wife, Ethel, who gave literary teas, murmured something about King Lear.

Role-Play
—Howard and Ethel at dinner with Pat
—Pat with two wealthy pastors from his seminary days
—Pat at a meeting with a group (the class) of professional men and women to discuss a fund drive.

Notebook Question

Page 8: Mao Zedong wrote, "Do not give the hungry man a fish. Give him a fishing pole." Suppose someone who was honestly starving came up to you. You have four dollars, and you give him two. The same thing happens tomorrow. And the next day. Finally, you come to the realization that the person's hunger is only the surface of the problem. What could you honestly, concretely, do to try to solve this problem on more than a today, surface level? (Don't talk about what you could do in the future. Talk about what you could do now, as you are.)

Meditation

There once was a man who, having had a good harvest from his land, thought to himself, "What am I to do? I haven't enough room to store my crops." Then he said, "This is what I'll do: I'll pull down my barns and build bigger ones, and store all my grain and my goods in them, and I'll say to my soul: 'My soul, you have plenty of good things laid by for many years to come. Take things easy. Eat, drink, and have a good time.' But God said to him, "Fool! This very night your soul will be required of you. And this hoard of yours? Whose will it be then?"

—Luke 12:16-21

As long as the readiness is there, a man is acceptable with whatever he can afford. Never mind what is beyond his means. This does not mean that to give relief to others you ought to make things difficult for yourselves. It is a question of balancing what happens to be your surplus now against their present need. And one day, they may have something to spare that will supply your needs.

—I Corinthians 9:12-15

They are surely wide of the mark who think that religion consists in acts of worship alone and in the discharge of certain moral obligations, and who imagine they can plunge themselves into earthly affairs in such a way as to imply that these are altogether divorced from the religious life. This split between the faith which many profess and their daily lives deserves to be counted among the more serious errors of our age.

—Vatican II, The Church Today

Unit 9

Conversions

The biggest disease today is not leprosy or tuberculosis,
but rather the feeling of being unwanted,
uncared for, and deserted by everybody. The greatest evil
is the lack of love and charity, the terrible indifference
toward one's neighbor who lives at the roadside, assaulted by exploitation,
corruption, poverty, and disease.

—*Mother Teresa*

Burlington, Vermont: Joe and Terry Powers worked at a boys' camp on the edge of Lake Champlain. In September, Joe was going to be a freshman at Holy Cross; Terry was going into senior year of high school. One night, after Joe had finally restored civilization to the Tadpole cabin, he was coming toward the cabin he and his brother shared and saw Terry with his pal, Donny Zweig, in the doorway, whispering. As Joe started up the path, Donny waved and took off for his own cabin. He called back to Terry, "Nine o'clock! Don't be late! It may take a coupla hours."

As Joe was getting ready for bed, he asked, "Where you two gonna spend your day off?"

Terry was hiding something; Joe could tell. "Oh, we thought we'd hitchhike up to Montreal," Terry said, a bit too airily.

"Where to in Montreal?"

"Oh, just this place Donny knows about." Joe sat down heavily on his bunk, his face screwed up at his kid brother. "You don't mean what I think you mean."

"What's wrong with it? Lotsa guys do it."

"How'd ya like Mom to find out?"

"She won't unless you tell her, and if you do, I'll tell her about that twenty bucks."

"That was only money. You're gonna use some girl like . . . like a thing."

"Get off it! We pay her twenty bucks apiece. It's a business."

"Well, it's also a sin, for one small thing."

"Listen, we talked about that. The commandment says, 'Thou shalt not commit *adultery*,' and neither of us is married."

"You're insane!"

"An' you're a *fag*!"

———

Bismarck, North Dakota: God had been good to Burt Lindstrom. He was a partner in the best law firm in the city; he had a wife who was not only still stunning at fifty-five, but who owned quite a busy boutique. His two girls were well married, and his son, Eric, was a high school senior. Eric was the kind of son every father hopes for and few get: intelligent, athletic, a lady-killer and, best of all, in charge of his school's service program. That made Burt proud. The kid cared about old people and retarded kids, and did something about it. He worked every summer with Indian kids on the reservation. That boy could apply to Harvard Law tomorrow! Burt was a lucky man, and he went to mass and communion every day of his life to thank God for his good life.

One evening, Eric rapped on the open door of his Dad's study. "Can I bend your ear a minute?"

"Sure, son, come on in. Sit down. As a matter of fact, I was just checking my portfolio to see how much we could afford next year. Not to worry. Sky's the limit."

"That's what I wanted to talk to you about, Dad. I know you want me to be a lawyer, but . . . ."

"Eric, I want you to be free to do what *you* want. What is it? Doctor? Professor? How about astronaut?"

"Dad, I want to work with the Indians." His father's jaw dropped open like a mailbox. Then he let out his breath with a hearty laugh. "For a minute there I thought you were *serious!*"

"I am serious, Dad."

"Eric, how the hell much money can you make doing that?"

The boy sat looking at the floor; he couldn't look up. "Dad, I want to be a priest."

It was as if his son had struck him. Burt got up from his desk. He needed to talk to his wife. He needed a drink.

"We'll talk about this later."

Albuquerque, New Mexico: Emilio Luna always had a good head for figures. Despite the fact that he had had to drop out of college, he had gotten a job in a bank, worked his way up, and had just been made a vice-president. It was a small bank, but Emilio was more than content.

Nita and Emilio Luna had not been able to have children of their own, so they had adopted two girls and a boy, each two years apart. But the day after Emilio moved into his new office, he and Nita decided that their good fortune was a sign from God: it was time to adopt another son.

The Lunas were no strangers at the orphanage of the Madonna de Los Angeles. Sister Dolores, the superior, met them in the lobby; her wise face wrinkled into smiles. "When you called, it was an answer to prayer. A boy! Come to the nursery! I want you to see him. A beauti-

ful boy." And when they got to the nursery, he was indeed beautiful.

But he was Vietnamese.

Nita looked at her husband a moment. Then she winked. "Well, there's not *that* much difference in the colors, is there?" Emilio grabbed his wife and swung her around, laughing.

"Such a happy moment," Sister Dolores sighed, "and such a sad one, too." The Lunas looked at her, puzzled. "He is the youngest of five in the same family, all here. The other four are girls."

Emilio looked at Nita. Together, they shrugged, then smiled.

"Okay!" Emilio chuckled. "God'll have to provide." Nita giggled back at him. "He should provide at least one brain between the two of us."

Pre-Test

A random collection of items and activities are listed below. Make four columns on a separate sheet of paper and label them: minimum life-style (essential), modest-but-adequate, comfortable, luxurious. In pencil (because you may want to rearrange), list the items in order of their relative importance to you as an individual when you're, say, ten years out of college. (The list isn't to impress anybody; the purpose is to give you insight, no one else. So be honest with yourself.)

Car	Travel	Color TV	Sports Tickets
TV (B/W)	Books	Refrigerator	Musical Instruments
Stove	Gifts to Needy	Records	Air Conditioning
Vacation	Vacation Home	2nd Car	Dinners Out
Boat	Watch	Stereo	2-Room Apartment
Food	Sports Car	Telephone	Tobacco
Pool	Typewriter	Cosmetics	Private Home
Insurance	Doctor/Dentist	Tuition	Sports Equipment

Almanac

The following are listed in terms of their average salaries. Number each profession in terms of service to the community. "1" signifies the most significant service.

_____ Tennis player	$1,682,850	_____ Comm. on Addiction	$38,771
_____ Anchorwoman	1,000,000	_____ English professor	38,475
_____ Pro bowler	134,7688	_____ NYC Sheriff	35,000
_____ Sec'y of State	80,000	_____ Air Traffic Controller	25,200
_____ Pres., Hairpiece Co.	75,000	_____ Government Nurse	22,840
_____ 20 yr. Admiral	74,000	_____ HS English Teacher	20,350
_____ Court of Appeals CJ	63,000	_____ Pharmacist	20,000
_____ Gov., California	49,100	_____ Cardinal of NYC	7,000

A Spectrum of Conversions

The Christian gospel is an unnerving call to conversion, from the values of the Kingdom of This World to the values of the Kingdom of Jesus Christ. If you want to put it more concretely: the Worldling is summed up in James Bond; the Christian is summed up in Mother Teresa of Calcutta. Guarding one's meager possessions is converted into its opposite: open-handedness.

Conversion is a U-turn—not necessarily a perfect reversal of achievements, but a reversal of *intentions*. But make no mistake about it: it is a *wrenching* experience. Those who are converted to Christianity later in life know that. But many "born Christians" never suffer conversion at all; to them, being Christian means being "nice," and usually only to one's friends.

Like the Kohlberg levels and stages we saw before, conversion does not usually happen by fits and starts; it is an *evolution*. And Jesus was not too much of a perfectionist to call on all the levels of motivation.

Stage 1: Fear of Punishment

Then I shall tell them to their faces: I have never known you. Away from me, you evil men. (Matthew 7:23)

The servant who knows what his master wants, but has not even started to carry out those wishes, will receive very many strokes of the lash. (Luke 12:47)

Stage 2: Hope of Reward

Come to me, all you who labor and are overburdened, and I will give you rest. (Matthew 11:28)

Do not judge, and you will not be judged yourself; do not condemn, and you will not be condemned yourselves; grant pardon and you will be pardoned. (Luke 6:37)

Stage 3: Group Loyalty

If your brother wrongs you seven times a day and seven times comes back to you and says, "I'm sorry," you must forgive him. (Luke 17:4)

If I then, the Lord and Master, have washed your feet, you should wash each other's feet. (John 13:14)

Stage 4: Law and Order

But to the man who told him (that his mother and brothers were outside), Jesus said, "Who is my mother? who are my brothers?" And stretching out his hand toward his disciples, he said, "Here are my mother and my brothers." (Matthew 12:48-49)

Stage 5: The Common Good

Do not suppose that I have come to bring peace to the earth. It is not peace I have come to bring, but a sword. (Matthew 19:34)

The sabbath was made for man, not man for the sabbath. (Mark 2:27)

Stage 6: Integrity/Wisdom

If anyone wants to be a follower of mine, let him renounce himself and take up his cross every day and follow me. For anyone who wants to save his life will lose it, but anyone who loses his life for my sake, that man will save it. (Luke 9:23-24)

There is one thing you lack. Go and sell everything you own and give the money to the poor, and you will have treasure in heaven; then come, follow me. (Mark 10:21)

Role-Play

There are six members of the Tenczar family:

Herb: the father, 53, ex-marine, sort-of successful lawyer, Kiwanis, member of the parish council, head usher.

Joyce: the mother, 51, homemaker, substitute grammar school teacher. Both Herb and Joyce have made a Marriage Encounter.

Fran: eldest daughter (or son), nun (or seminarian), who has recently left religious life but remained a practicing Catholic.

Sandy: high school junior (boy or girl), captain of the basketball team, B + student, no real trouble so far.

Nat: sixth grade, winner of the top academics and religion prizes every year for five years.

Grandma: lives in a government subsidized apartment for senior citizens, refusing to live with her children for fear, as she says, "I keep you people from making the same mistakes I learned from."

Role-Play

Full family dinner. Sandy has just declared that she (or he) is bored stiff with the parish Mass and won't go again—even if it means being grounded till Doomsday.

Notebook Question

Page 9: Go back and look at your chart from the Pre-Test. Of the thirty-two items, what number was "Gifts to Needy" for you. Try to explain why it had that position relative to the other items.

Meditation

Do not model yourselves on the behavior of the world around you, but let your behavior change, modeled by your new mind. This is the only way to discover the will of God and know what is good, what it is God wants, what is the perfect thing to do.

—Romans 12:2

It was for the common use of all human beings, rich and poor, that the earth was created. Why then do the rich claim for themselves a monopoly in the ownership of the land? Nature knows nothing of rich men. All her children are born into nakedness and poverty, and bring with them into the world neither gold nor silver. Therefore, the alms you give to a poor man is not yours to give; you are restoring to him a portion of what is his own.

—Saint Ambrose

There is a growing awareness of the exalted dignity proper to the human person, since he stands above all things, and his rights and duties are universal and inviolable. Therefore, there must be available to all men everything necessary for leading a life truly human, such as food, clothing, and shelter; the right to choose a state of life freely and to found a family, the right to education, to employment, to a good reputation, to respect, to appropriate information, to activity in accord with the upright norm of one's own conscience, to protection of privacy and to rightful freedom in matters of religion.

The ferment of the gospel has aroused and continues to arouse in human hearts the irresistible requirements of human dignity.

—Vatican II, The Church Today

Part II

The Practice of Justice

Unit 10

Group Homicide

Yahweh asked Cain, "Where is your brother, Abel?"
And Cain replied, "I do not know. Am I my brother's keeper?"
Yahweh asked, "What have you done? Listen! The voice
of your brother's blood cries to me from the earth!"
—*Genesis 4:9-10*

Houston, Texas: The Savage Nomads were Number One! Since Bobo had become Prez and made Stilt the War Counselor and Whip the Armorer, no member of a rival gang had dared to cross Western Avenue into their turf. It had not taken long, either. Stilt had good ideas: never go for the rival Prez; go for his family or his chick. Once a few of the opposition's sisters got their legs broken, those mothers *learned.*

Two new problems had arisen: first, expansion; new turf was always needed; new storeowners to pay insurance for their windows. Second was Ortiz. Ortiz was a pimp; no great hassle, except he'd recruited two Nomad girls.

Stilt laid out the plans, a small, tight operation. Bobo and Freak were to use Molotov cocktails on Ortiz's old lady's *bodega;* Whip and Needle were to rape Ortiz's sister, slice her if necessary; and Stilt and Gunsel were to get Ortiz and his fag boy.

Stilt loved the Nomads. It was

. . . structured, neat; it ran like a family should run. He had no compunction about what he did. Stilt had been savaged by his drunk of an old man since he was in the crib box. It was the way you got what you wanted.

By one a.m. Saturday morning it was all over. The *bodega* was torched, and Carmela Ortiz was moaning in an alley off Fox Street. In another alley, Stilt and Gunsel tied Ortiz and his chicken to the railing of a fire escape. They had castrated the boy and then stabbed him twice in the chest. They did nothing to Ortiz. Except make him watch.

Stilt was proud. He felt like a man. And even if the cops from the 41st picked him up, no hassle. The most he could get was eighteen months. Because Stilt was only fifteen years old.

Belfast, Northern Ireland: Agnes McGurk ran a quiet little pub in the

New Lodge Road. It was a rundown place, you could say, but a lovely bit of a place where the old fellas and their wives could have a pint in peace and watch the telly or play a game of darts. None of the youngsters and none of that jungle music at McGurk's.

Agnes had not had the easy life—twelve children by the age of thirty-eight. Two died young; half her eight sons and two of her daughters had emigrated. Jerry, who was twenty-eight, was in the Maze, sentenced to eighteen years for a raid on a jail trying to free two IRA men. He was a tough kid, our Jerry.

It was after supper one night in the middle of December, and the old lads and their missuses were jawing about Christmas and Christmases past, like the time Kieran Boylan had pinched Monsignor O'Hanlon's turkey and given it to the Poor Clares as a present from the Holy Name Society.

Then, suddenly, almost at closing time, the talk of Christmases was silenced in the thunder of fifty-eight pounds of gelignite which a man in a long overcoat had placed by the side door.

When the dust had settled and the fire lorries had withdrawn, it was not an easy task for the lads from Mercy Hospital. Bits and pieces, really. Most of the old folks had died of burns and suffocation. But when the pub collapsed, the gas mains must have exploded. Only two or three had been dismembered by the gelignite itself. It was a gas explosion mostly.

It was an odd thing, though. The bombers hadn't known anything about Jerry McGurk, who was an IRA lad like themselves. They were really aiming at Flaherty's bar three miles up the road. But they couldn't make it in time before closing. So they left the stuff at the first pub they came to before closing time. Actually, it didn't make that much difference now, did it?

Washington, DC: On April 22, 1971, Navy Lieutenant John Kerry sat in his wheelchair before the Senate Foreign Relations Committee investigating Vietnam veterans' grievances. At twenty-five, Kerry would never walk again. He was finding it difficult to explain the war to the senators. How does one explain, to one who has never lived it, what it does to a man's nerves to listen, taut, every minute of the day for a year, for the snap of a grenade fuse or the whoosh of a mortar that will turn him into a basket case?

He explained that in Vietnam soldiers committed crimes on a day-to-day basis, with the full awareness of officers at all levels of command. "Men raped," he testified, "cut off ears and heads, taped wires from field telephones to human genitals and turned up the power, cut off limbs, blew up bodies, poisoned food supplies." And it was all done in the name of some "mystical war on communism," even though most of the people didn't even know the difference between communism and democracy. They practiced the art of survival, siding with whichever military force was present at a particular time.

And the American soldiers rationalized, destroying villages in order to save them, working in "free-fire zones," which meant you shot anything that moved, especially if it were Oriental. There was a glorification of "body counts" in which officer vied with officer for the greatest number, as long as they were Orientals.

Two million people had died to prove that America couldn't lose a war. Now, Kerry said, one out of every ten unemployed Americans was a Vietnam veteran; 57% of those entering VA hospitals talked of suicide; 27% had tried it.

"How," Lieutenant Kerry asked, "do we pacify our own hearts?"

Pre-Test

Indicate the degree of your approval or disapproval of the following statements.

1. The aggression which is, in some degree, in every one of us is instinctive from birth and not programmed into us by our upbringing. $\qquad$ +2 $\qquad$ +1 $\qquad$ −1 $\qquad$ −2

2. If people like Stilt are brutal criminals without consciences, society has to take at least some of the blame. $\qquad$ +2 $\qquad$ +1 $\qquad$ −1 $\qquad$ −2

3. Terrorist groups have to resort to extreme measures to correct injustices, just as parents have to punish children in order to make them act justly.   +2   +1   −1   −2

4. The war in Vietnam was, in many senses, an international version of Stilt's street activities.   +2   +1   −1   −2

5. At the very least, the two million deaths in the Vietnam War proved to the communists that we would not allow them to win easily.   +2   +1   −1   −2

6. In order to conclude a just war, it is justifiable to use at least small tactical nuclear weapons.   +2   +1   −1   −2

7. If nothing else, war settles down many young men, gives them discipline, loyalty to a common purpose, and manliness.   +2   +1   −1   −2

8. Since there is no way of telling which conscientious objectors are sincere and which are cowards, all who refuse to enlist should be punished.   +2   +1   −1   −2

9. If Russia were to move troops into Quebec to assist the French-speaking separatists, American troops should be sent in to assist our long-time Canadian ally.   +2   +1   −1   −2

10. If there were camps in Brazil to exterminate the remaining Indians, and if all other attempts at negotiation and economic reprisal failed, the United States would not only be justified but obligated to send in troops to rescue the Indians.   +2   +1   −1   −2

Almanac

Again, pencil in your guesses before you look up the answers in the Almanac.

1. How many men and women served in the Armed Forces during the Vietnam War?   1._____

2. How many died in battle?   2._____

3. How many were wounded?   3._____

4. What are the three states with the highest crime rates?   4.(A)_____

(B)_____

(C)_____

5.   What are the three cities with the highest crime rates?

5.(A)_____

(B)_____

(C)_____

6.   How many males under eighteen were arrested last year for:

Murder _____

Forcible rape _____

Larceny-theft _____

DWI _____

Total _____

7.   How many public figures in the world were assassinated between:

1863-1883 _____

1963-1983 _____

The Man He Killed

Had he and I but met
By some old ancient inn,
We should have sat us down to wet
Right many a nipperkin!*   *Glass of liquor

But ranged as infantry,
And staring face to face,
I shot at him as he at me,
And killed him in his place.

I shot him dead because—
Because he was my foe,
Just so: my foe of course he was;
That's clear enough; although

He thought he'd list,* perhaps,   *Enlist
Off-hand like—just as I—
Was out of work—had sold his traps—
No other reason why.

Yes; quaint and curious war is!
You shoot a fellow down
You'd treat if met where any bar is,
Or help to half-a-crown.*   *About a dollar

—*Thomas Hardy*

Role-Play

Everybody agreed that Ernie Tauber was a bit weird. Not that he was clinically insane, but he did some pretty bizarre things to get attention. He won five dollar bets like swallowing a small mouse live or drinking a bottle of ink; things like that. One evening, somewhat against his parents' wishes, Chris Cook went over to Ernie's house to study for a biology exam. Chris was a pretty level-headed kid, but he was fascinated by Ernie Tauber and, for some reason, Ernie was a whiz in biology.

While they were upstairs, ostensibly studying, Ernie suddenly yanked open his desk drawer and pulled out his father's revolver. Chris was frozen in panic, but Ernie laughed and said, "It's not loaded, you sissy! See?" He pointed the gun at Chris's head and pulled the trigger. The bullet tore off the left side of Chris's head.

It is now 12:38 a.m. The Cooks have just returned from the hospital where their son was pronounced dead on arrival. They are sitting around the kitchen trying to decide what to do.

Role-play

Sam: the father, 48, insurance salesman, Little League umpire, former college hockey All-American; open, hearty, hard drinking;

Anne: the mother, 44, her husband's secretary and bookkeeper, a very nervous woman who once had a nervous breakdown;

Rich: 22, truck driver and mechanic, dropped out of college after one semester; semi-pro hockey player; steady, loyal, but hot-tempered;

Sue: 18, high school senior, best friend of Ernie Tauber's sister, Julie, who is mortified by her brother's "strangeness."

Notebook Question

Page 10: If the President of the United States declared war on a Middle Eastern country because it had interrupted the flow of oil to the United States and fired on two American ships, sinking them and killing most of their crews, what would be your reaction to an induction notice?

Meditation

Yahweh will wield authority over the nations and adjudicate between many peoples; these will hammer their swords into plowshares, their spears into sickles. Nation will not lift sword against nation, there will be no more training for war.

—Isaiah 2:4

But we should not let false hope deceive us. For enmities and hatred must be put away and firm, honest agreements concerning world peace reached in the future. Otherwise, for all its marvelous knowledge, humanity, which is already in the middle of a grave crisis, will perhaps be brought to that mournful hour in which it will experience no peace other than the dreadful peace of death.

—Vatican II, The Church Today

Unit 11

Who's in Charge of Life and Death?

You have heard how it was said to our ancestors:
'You shall not kill,'
but I say this to you: anyone who is angry
with his brother will answer for it.
—*Matthew 6:21*

Florida State Penitentiary: Bobby Lee Davis had been living on death row for seven years. It had been seven years of appeals, all the way to the Supreme Court, which refused to hear the case. Bobby Lee had no more hope. The governor had already reprieved him three times. He was due to die in twenty-four hours.

Eight years before, Bobby Lee had been accused of killing a white housewife named Joanna Friel in her kitchen while he was delivering her groceries. There had been two eyewitnesses. The first witness, the victim's brother, Frank, an epileptic, testified that a black boy, whom he identified as Bobby Lee Davis, had struck Mrs. Friel across the face. At the moment, the witness had had an epileptic seizure, breaking his watch in the fall. The time was 2:43 p.m.

The other witness had been Mrs. Ida Glenroy, a black woman who lived across the street from the Friel home. (Neighbors testified that if Ida missed anything that hap-pened in the neighborhood, it hadn't happened.) Mrs. Glenroy testified that she had seen Bobby Lee Davis exit the Friel house at 2:45. She was certain of the time because it was during the middle commercial of "The Guiding Light," and she had paused momentarily to part her curtains "to be sure none of the neighborhood children was in trouble."

Both witnesses and several juries had been certain beyond reasonable doubt.

Bobby Lee Davis died in the electric chair still protesting his innocence. His confessor, Fr. Joseph Gelardo, was also certain that Bobby Lee was innocent, but he had no way to present his confidential evidence.

Mt. Vernon, Illinois: At the Farrell's barbecue, Carol Irving was helping Ginny Farrell fast-defrost more ham-burger from the freezer. The kids were ravenous today. Ginny had known Carol for four years, and she knew something was wrong. She kept trying to peel off the soft from the frozen meat when suddenly she dropped the whole mess in the luke-warm water, "Okay, Carol. Spill it! This sweet grinning silence is driving me nuts!"

Carol Irving sat down in the kitchen chair as if she'd been struck. She began to cry. "Oh, my God, Ginny, I'm pregnant again."

Ginny ran to kneel at her side and hugged her friend. "Oh, Carol, I thought it was something awful! This is wonderful. You have two beautiful little boys. Now you're going to have a beautiful little girl. I just know it!"

Carol looked up, her face streaked with tears. "No. Mark says we can't afford it. He made an appointment for me on Monday."

Ginny Farrell stood up, slowly, hardly breathing. Just then Scotty Irving ran in on his way to the john and saw his mother crying. Wordlessly, he came over and just put his hand on his mother's shoulder. Ginny Farrell grabbed up a long knife from the sink top. "Carol," she said, grimly, "stick this in Scotty's back."

Carol stood up, thunderstruck. Scotty ran out of the room. "Are you *insane?*"

Ginny sagged against the sink. "No. At least Scotty could run away."

Memphis, Tennessee: Liz Harrison had been in St. Jude's Hospital for Children for two years. She was fourteen years old. At twelve, she had been in an accident in a car driven by her brother, Jody, seventeen. Jody had been killed instantly; Liz had not recovered consciousness since the accident. Her thin body was fed and emptied by a forest of tubes and wires—intravenous feeding, heartlung machine, catheter. There was no brain activity whatever.

The doctors had tried everything. Norm and Lois Harrison could not fault that. The Harrisons had brought in other doctors from all over the country and one from Montreal. They had trusted; they had prayed. But the medical care, even with donations from all over the state, had nearly impoverished them. They had three more little children. And still Liz lay there, blinking, her chest moving quietly, but it was not Liz.

Last Saturday evening, Norm Harrison sent his wife home early; she was exhausted. The nasal, plastic voice of the PA system told visitors that visiting hours were over. Norm Harrison knelt by the side of his daughter's bed and said an act of contrition. Then he rose, pulled out every single wire and tube from her body, and left the hospital, weeping quietly.

Pre-Test

Indicate the extent of your agreement or disagreement with each of the following.

1. Life is not as precious to those who are deprived of quality lives (retarded, comatose, crippled, poor, vicious criminals) as to those with more varied lives.   +2   +1   −1   −2

2. With the extensive appeals allowed to a capital criminal—all the way to the Supreme Court—there is very little likelihood that an innocent convict would be executed in the United States.   +2   +1   −1   −2

3. It is "cruel and unusual punishment" to keep a convicted murderer cooped up on death row for what might be fifty years. It is more humane to execute him or her and get it over with.   +2   +1   −1   −2

4. The amount of money spent on a death row criminal in the course of his or her lifetime—money spent by the very society the criminal victimized—is reason enough in itself to execute the criminal.   +2   +1   −1   −2

5. Ginny Farrell's instinctive reaction to Carol Irving's decision for an abortion was melodramatic and cruel.

+ 2	+ 1	− 1	− 2

6. The Supreme Court has the right and obligation to give final judgments on both legality and morality for citizens of the United States.

+ 2	+ 1	− 1	− 2

7. Even though a girl is a minor in all other respects (drinking, voting, and so on), an unwanted pregnancy is so humiliating that she should be allowed to obtain an abortion without her parents' knowledge.

+ 2	+ 1	− 1	− 2

8. Norm Harrison should be prosecuted and convicted for the premeditated homicide of his daughter.

+ 2	+ 1	− 1	− 2

9. The right of science to search for medical information that will help future generations of human beings justifies keeping terminally ill patients alive after "brain death" in order to develop new methods of saving lives.

+ 2	+ 1	− 1	− 2

10. If a victim of "brain death" is taken off support machines but still continues to live, physicians are then justified in giving the patient drugs that will cause or hasten death.

+ 2	+ 1	− 1	− 2

Almanac

1. (A) How many abortions took place in the United States this year?

(A)_____

(B) What percentage of them were for women under 20?

(B)_____

(C) What percentage for unmarried women?

(C)_____

2. In terms of casualties (dead and wounded), which were the two costliest wars America ever fought?

2._____

_____

3. What were the most recent United States statistics on the number of:

Violent crimes: _____

Murders: _____

Forcible rapes: _____

4. (A) How many men and women are in state and federal prisons?

(A)_____

(B) How many of those are on death rows?

(B)_____

5. In what five-year age-range are the most suicides in the United States?

5._____

Role-Play

Nancy Paulino and Steve Cummings, both high school seniors, have been going together for two years. It's been a stormy relationship; the two of them are very strong-willed and their fights are sometimes minor epics. For weeks afterward, they won't see each other or try to talk, each waiting for the other to phone, half-tempted to call but willing to wait for the other one to see the light and beg forgiveness. Somehow, though, they have always gradually drifted back together and, for awhile, they are inseparable. For the last four months, at least during their "together" phases, they have slept together at least eight or ten times. It has not been more frequent because Nancy was not too keen on it; but Steve pleaded, insisted, and finally got his way each time.

Two weeks ago, Nancy and Steve had their worst fight yet. She had not had her period. They were both terrified and took out their anger at themselves on one another. She blamed him for being so selfish; and he blamed her for not taking the pill, especially since he'd been willing to pay for them.

Today Nancy's doctor confirmed that she is indeed pregnant. They have four options: (A) have an abortion; (B) get married; (C) have Nancy go away, have the baby, and give it up for adoption; (D) Nancy have the child and remain single.

Role-Play
—each with the school nurse or counselor
—each with one of their parents
—Steve with Nancy's father
—the two mothers or fathers
—Nancy with a girl who's had an abortion.

Notebook Question

Page 11: In the preceding role-play situation (A) which of the four options do you honestly believe is the most just, and give your reasons; and (B) which do you think you would personally choose if you were actually in the situation yourself, and give your reasons?

Meditation

Then the chief priests and Pharisees called a meeting. "Here is this man working all these signs," they said, "and what action are we taking? If we let him go on his way, everybody will believe in him, and the Romans will come and destroy the Holy Place and our nation."

One of them, Caiphas, the high priest that year, said, "You don't seem to have grasped the situation at all; you fail to see that it is better for one man to die for the people, than for the whole nation to be destroyed."

—John 11:47-51

Tomorrow and tomorrow and tomorrow
Creeps in this petty pace from day to day
To the last syllable of recorded time,
And all our yesterdays have lighted fools
The way to dusty death. Out, out, brief candle!
Life's but a walking shadow, a poor player
That struts and frets his hour upon the stage
And then is heard no more. It is a tale
Told by an idiot, full of sound and fury,
Signifying nothing.

—William Shakespeare

Unit 12

The Race Race

If you prick us, do we not bleed? If you
tickle us, do we not laugh? If you poison us, do we not die?
And if you wrong us, shall we not revenge? If we
are like you in the rest, we will resemble you in that.
—*William Shakespeare*

Pima Reservation, Arizona: On February 19, 1945, the U.S. Marines landed on the tiny island of Iwo Jima. Nobody had ever heard of it before; it was only nine square miles, the smallest of the islands in the Japanese archipelago. But it was the stepping stone to a landing in April on the much larger island of Okinawa, 400 miles south of the main islands. A group of Marines braved their way up a hilltop to muscle upright a pole with the American flag, and they were caught in an unforgettable photograph by Jim Rosenthal. Later, that heroic act was immortalized in bronze and became the U.S. Marine Memorial in Arlington Cemetery. That cluster of ragged men seemed to embody all that the Marine Corps stood for—and all that America found best in itself.

One of those men was an American Indian, Ira Hayes. He returned stateside to a breathtaking hero's welcome—medals, parades, bond rallies, receptions—every means

American society could use to show its gratitude.

Then the parades ended. Ira returned to the Pima Reservation. He could find no work. He became a new symbol. He was now the typical Indian. Forgotten. He became an alcoholic. No battles now, no job, no hope. One night, Ira Hayes, hero of Iwo Jima, dead drunk, fell into a drainage ditch and drowned in two inches of water.

———

Brooklyn, New York: Attie Johnson has lived in the Brownsville section of Brooklyn for three years; before that, it was Newark; before that "somewheres else." She feels shamed living on welfare, but she has five kids, four too young for school. She is only twenty-three years old, and no husband around, so "They's worse things than shame; my babies dyin'd be worse."

Attie Johnson has no hard feelings against her husband. She knows the way things are. "No," she says quietly, "the black guy just don't sit down one day and figure out how much his wife and kids is gonna receive from the welfare after he skips. He pulls out 'cause the family has a rough time makin' ends meet on his salary. He come home at night and it's nag, nag, nag. 'We need this. We need that.' We'd both get aggravated over what we needed and couldn't buy, and we'd start at one another's throats again. I had a bit of a job then, and he didn't have none; so it kinda got to him that he was, you know, livin' off me. One day I come home and he'd packed his stuff and left two dollars for me."

———

Billings, Montana: This week it was sugar beets. Ricio Alvarez, his wife, and six children have a '62 Ford pick-up. For many months it is their home, traveling from Brownsville, Texas, where they came over the border, to New Mexico, to California, and north to Oregon and Montana, following the harvest, wherever there is rumor in the camps that there is work up ahead. They live the life of permanent strangers.

Stoop-work is hard under the hot sun, and the hours are long, since the crops must be picked when they are ripe. The money is not good. But enough to keep going. And going. Four of the children are now over eight and old enough to help; the other two go to school for the three or four days wherever they stop, as their brothers and sisters did. They don't like it; the children laugh at their clothes and bare feet, and they can hardly make out what the teacher says in English. But it frees the mother to work.

Last night, near the back of the truck, the oldest boy walked out of the dark into the pale light from the kerosene lamp on the tailgate. He put his hand on his father's sleeve and asked, "Papa, do I have to grow up like you?"

Pre-Test

Indicate the extent of your aggreement or disagreement with the following.

1. Ira Hayes was gutless.	+2	+1	−1	−2
2. Attie Johnson should have beaten her husband to it and left him with the kids.	+2	+1	−1	−2
3. Ricio Alvarez is responsible for the situation his family is in.	+2	+1	−1	−2
4. Because the Indians were wasting vast valuable lands, Europeans were justified in taking it away for the common good.	+2	+1	−1	−2
5. If you have very large acreage around your home, and a ghetto family is sleeping ten in a room, they have a right to pitch a tent on your land.	+2	+1	−1	−2
6. If Arab oil sheiks are willing and able to pay twice as much as Americans for hundreds of thousands of acres of American land, the owners should sell to them rather than to Americans at lower prices.	+2	+1	−1	−2
7. When it comes to entering college, middle-class whites profit from the fact that very many blacks and others are poorly trained to take the SAT's.	+2	+1	−1	−2
8. If a registered adult immigrant speaks only a foreign language, he or she should be subsidized by the government to go to school—as native-born children do—to learn the language before having to find a job.	+2	+1	−1	−2

9. Jesus did not ask anyone to impoverish himself or herself; but, in the name of justice, we may have to do with less than we'd expected or felt entitled to.   + 2   + 1   − 1   − 2

10. If a cripple is in a race, in fairness, he or she should be given a head start.   + 2   + 1   − 1   − 2

Almanac

Pencil in rough guesses before looking up the answers.

1. Salaries: Fill in the *top* income for each fifth of the U.S. population:

	Lowest	Second	Third	Fourth	Top
Total	_____	_____	_____	_____	_____
White	_____	_____	_____	_____	_____
Black	_____	_____	_____	_____	_____

2. Education: Using only those individuals twenty-five years or older, find the number of people and percentage of educational attainment:

	All persons	% Less than HS	% High School	% College
White males	_____	_____	_____	_____
White females	_____	_____	_____	_____
Black males	_____	_____	_____	_____
Black females	_____	_____	_____	_____
Hispanic males	_____	_____	_____	_____
Hispanic females	_____	_____	_____	_____

3. What five states have the highest Indian unemployment, that is, Indians over 16 seeking work but still jobless? [All over 50%]

(A)_____

(B)_____

(C)_____

(D)_____

(E)_____

dis-crim-i-na′tion

n.   1.   Act of discriminating, or state of being discriminated.
2.   That which discriminates; a mark of distinction.   3.   The quality of being discriminating; faculty of nicely distinguishing.
4.   A distinction, as in treatment; esp. an unfair or injurious distinction.

© Washington Post Writers Group

Role-Play

Divide into pairs. In each pair, one is a social worker, the other is either Ira Hayes before his death, or Attie Johnson, or Ricio Alvarez. Let the individual declare his or her life situation and needs to the social worker, then let the social worker give the best advice he or she can give. If there is any pair that feels they have come up with something worthwhile, let them do it again in front of everybody.

Notebook Question

Page 12: By this time, whether taken altogether or even in one or other of its parts, all of this must be starting to get a little depressing. On this page, try to exorcise that depression. On the one hand, it is a very good thing; it is a sign of compassion. On the other hand, it is a very sad thing; it makes you feel lousy about something which, at least at the moment, you can do nothing about. Reflect not only on the reasons why opening up such questions is good, but also on what safeguards you have to take to insure that it's not overwhelming.

Meditation

You have stripped off your old behavior with your old self, and you have put on a new self which will progress toward true knowledge the more it is renewed in the image of its creator. And in that image there is no room for distinction between Greek and Jew, between circumcised or uncircumcised, or between barbarian and Scythian, slave and free man. There is only Christ; he is everything and he is in everything.

—Colossians 3:10-11

True, all human beings are not alike from the point of view of varying physical power and the diversity of intellectual and moral resources. Nevertheless, with respect to the *fundamental* rights of the person, every type of discrimination—whether social or cultural, whether based on sex, race, color, social condition, language, or religion—is to be overcome and eradicated as contrary to God's intent.

—Vatican II, The Church Today

Unit 13

Sex as a Weapon

"She is my goods, my chattels, she is my house,
My household stuff, my field, my bard,
My horse, my ox, my ass, my anything."
—*William Shakespeare*
A woman, without a man, is like a fish without a bicycle.
—*Gloria Steinem*

Boston, Massachusetts: If Ruth Clifford heard, "You're overqualified," one more time, she was ready to commit mayhem. For four years at Smith she had enslaved herself to books and cloistered herself in the library so that the little girl from Liberal, Kansas, could march into the personnel office of Bache and Co. or Merrill Lynch and show them the Barbara Walters of stockbrokers. Several personnel men invited her out to dinner (with perhaps a few options afterwards), but no job offers. She tried going without make-up, wearing frumpy clothes; still no job. Not even any invitations.

Finally, after four months of TV dinners in a $175 apartment where the john didn't work, Ruth Clifford, *summa cum laude* from Smith College, accepted a position as receptionist and secretary with the Fitzwell Girdle Company of Needham, Massachusetts.

Philadelphia, Pennsylvania: Elena Aguilar is a tiny, once pretty young woman who came with her man from Puerto Rico two years ago. They had one child each year in the five years they were living together. Two weeks ago, Jorge did not come home from looking for work. Elena was terrified. She thought of going to the priest, but was afraid he would be angry because she had five children and had never been married. She went to the welfare office, but the lady, even though she spoke Spanish, was very busy and very surly. The questions the lady asked about Elena and Jorge were so embarrassing, and what the lady said and the forms were so confusing that Elena fled in tears.

There was no food left for the children. There was only $3.93 in the envelope in the cupboard under the dishes. Elena put on a peasant blouse that Jorge had never allowed her to wear except in the house, for him. She took the money and went to the Woolworth's. There she bought a pair of big spangle earrings and a dark red lipstick. She was not good at making up, but she tried very hard, though her hand was shaking and the crying kept making the mascara run down her cheeks.

The man who stopped her on Market St. was a big man in working clothes on his lunch break. He smelled bad and he hadn't shaved. He took her to a dirty hotel. She kept saying her children's names, over and over, over, and over.

Madison, Wisconsin: Dave Egan had always been the jock of the family. His high school football coach said, in public, at the year-end Sports Award Banquet in his senior year, that Dave was the best all-around athlete he'd ever coached and one of the finest gentlemen it had ever been his privilege to teach. Dave had to fend off college scouts like offensive linemen. He settled on the University of Wisconsin because, even

97

though the competition would be tougher, if he made it, there would be lots of publicity at home, and his Dad wanted more than anything else for his son to play for Green Bay. And Joe Egan seldom failed to get what he wanted.

Dave's college career had been excellent. In junior year he was first-string quarterback, almost certain to be Big Ten MVP.

And then the roof fell in. The night the season ended, after a gala drunk with the team, Dave Egan's roommate found him in bed with a sophomore tackle.

Dave had always known. He'd tried so hard to fight against it. But that night nothing had mattered. At 4:00 p.m. his roommate found him again, in the bathroom, with his forearms razored from the wrist to the elbow.

Pre-Test

Indicate whether you believe each of the following statements to be true or false.

1. Sex is connected to justice only by the negative laws of God and society against sexual indulgence. True False

2. The Bill of Rights gave women the full rights of citizenship. True False

3. Women have representation in Congress proportionate to their percentage of the American population. True False

4. Women have less stamina and care for detail than men. True False

5. For thousands of years women were considered to be a man's most valuable goods and means of production. True False

6. Women are paid less for doing the same jobs men do. True False

7. Most prostitutes chose "the oldest profession" because they enjoy the work. True False

8. Men and women choose to be homosexual the same way others choose to be heterosexual. True False

9. Homosexuality is highest in countries that tolerate it openly and lowest in countries where the "macho" image is the ideal. True False

10. Homosexuals can easily be recognized by their obvious effeminacy. True False

Almanac

Remembering that women make up over half the population of the United States, (half of 225 million):

1. Of the 100 U.S. Senators, how many are women?

    1._____

2. Of the 435 Representatives, how many women?

    2._____

3. Of the 13 cabinet members, how many women?

    3._____

4. Of the 186 Justices who have served on the Supreme Court, how many have been women?

    4._____

5. At present, how many governors are women?

    5._____

6. In the index of employed persons, of the twelve million managers/administrators, how many women?

    6._____

7. In the past year, how many prostitution arrests:

	Total	Under 18
Males	_____	_____
Females	_____	_____

Staking Sexual Claims

—"Aw, come on, honey! I've taken you out for two months now. You gotta let me!"

—"Jimmy, we've been going together for two months now. Don't you think it's time we talked about going steady?"

—"We went to your parents last Christmas. This year we're going to mine."

—"So we don't have any kids. We've lived together for ten years! You can't walk out on me now!"

"Suppose you did own him. Could you really love somebody who was absolutely nobody without you? You really want somebody like that? Somebody who falls apart when you walk out the door? You don't, do you? And neither does he. You're turning over your whole life to him. Your whole life, girl. And if it means so little to you that you can just give it away, hand it to him, then why should it mean any more to him? He can't value you more than you value yourself."

—*Toni Morrison*

The Little Women

Men have broad and large chests and small narrow hips and are more understanding than women, who have small and narrow chests and broad hips, and to that end they should remain at home, sit still, keep house, and bring up children.

—*Martin Luther*

Prostitution

In a book called *Hellhole*, Sara Harris quotes a forty-six-year-old prostitute with a partial elementary education on her twenty-eighth commitment to the New York City House of Detention:

> And sometimes, most of the time in fact, the ladies I used to clean house for act like I am a crook. Some of them examine in my bag to see if I toting things. But a couple examine me all over like I'm in court or in the House of D.; and they one madam, she make me take off my dress and show her if I got anything hid underneath. And to shake out my shoes. And I got all shook up while shaking out my shoes and I say to myself, 'All the prostitutes I know ain't no worse off than I who try to do a honest job, to take care of me and my baby.' So with everything, I just don't care. I mean what I remember about my first trick is I remember he pay me $1.25 to go up on a roof, and he a white man all dressed up in a blue suit and wearing a tie, and if he ever tell a white woman to do what he tell me to do for $1.25, she kill him.

Homosexuality

Psychological researcher Dr. C. A. Tripp, who interviewed over seven hundred homosexuals and scores of field anthropologists all over the world draws several conclusions:

1. Sexual preferences are not hereditary or explicitly chosen; they are learned. It is not a choice, any more than liking breasts more than legs or blondes more than brunettes. A powerful homosexual conditioning usually begins at such an early age that the child is often more aware of pressures against heterosexuality than against homosexuality.

2. Homosexuality has a higher ratio in macho and competitive societies (cf. Greece and Rome) and doesn't rise much above zero in societies that eschew heroics and thus take the glory out of maleness.

3. Only a fraction of homosexuals are effeminate. More than 90% of them show no effeminacy at all.

Role-Play

ARC, Cessna Aircraft's avionics division, is seeking an experienced Manager of Technical Publications for a new branch in Saudi Arabia. All applicants should be degreed with several years of managerial responsibility and possess the written and oral communicative skills necessary to interface effectively in this area.

Finalists:

MAUREEN KRAMER, 32, 5'6", 128 lbs., married to an adman (Roote, Jacobsen); two children, 8 and 6; licensed pilot; bachelor of Fine Arts (minor in Semitic languages) Pratt Institute, *cum laude.*
Comments: Interviewer found Mrs. Kramer very poised, articulate, self-assured.

JOHN OATES, 30, 6'0", 175 lbs., married, no children; taking flying lessons; MFA Rochester Institute of Technology, cumulative: 3.6.

Comments: Mr. Oates is a well-spoken black man whose wife is Lebanese; he speaks some Arabic but cannot read it.

JAY DENBY, 36, 6'4", 215 lbs., single; bomber pilot in Vietnam; AB pre-law from Georgetown U., *magna cum laude.*
Comments: The interviewer is not sure of his judgment. Mr. Denby seems quite manly, but perhaps a bit too impeccably dressed and seems a man of very expensive tastes, jewelry, etc.

Role-Play
Three-person board at which each of the three final candidates is interviewed once more; after that, the panel discusses and makes a final choice.

Notebook Question

Page 13: Is there any group of people who have been mentioned in the last two units whom, even against your best intentions, you find difficulty feeling much real sympathy for? If so, try to explain why. If there is not, is there any group of people you find "just a bit too hard to take"?

Meditation

Set me like a seal on your heart,
like a seal on your arm.
For love is strong as Death,
jealousy as relentless as the Underworld.
The flash of it is a flash of fire,
a flame of Yahweh himself.
Love no flood can quench, no torrent drown.

—Song of Songs 8:6

Women are now employed in almost every area of life. It is appropriate that they should be able to assume their full proper role in accordance with their own nature. Everyone should acknowledge and favor the proper and necessary participation of women in cultural life.

—Vatican II, The Church Today

Unit 14

Criminal Justice

> If any of you gentlemen own dogs, you're treating them
> better than we're treated here.
> —Attica Inmate, 1971

Darien, Connecticut: At St. Bernard's High, they called Diane Coleman "The Queen Bee." Nobody fussed with Diane. She was, as even many of her intimates admitted, "a cold-hearted bitch." Someplace in her head, she kept a kind of file that recorded everything she saw or heard about any girl in the school. And whenever she wanted some information, or whenever she was preparing one of her "good-hearted, madcap pranks" on a teacher, or trying to cover it up, she invariably found a tidbit that could reduce any obstacle to tears and eager conformity.

Then she blew up the chem lab. It was sort of a warning to prissy old Mrs. Ayler that Diane should not be flunked again. Ever. But Pam Metzler knew. She had proof. And forthrightly, stupidly, she told the principal. Diane was suspended for two weeks, and during that time Diane went through that mental file and added up all the debts. Then she got on the phone.

For seven months of senior year, from October 28 to June 6, no girl at St. Bernard's spoke to Pam Metzler, even on the phone. Their boyfriends were enlisted, too. Pam was sentenced to "The Silence." Justice will be done.

Auschwitz, Poland: Fr. Maximilian Kolbe, OFM, had been the newspaper apostle of Poland for many years. Too many years. On February 17, 1941, he was taken to Dachau prison near Munich, Germany, and soon after shipped back to Auschwitz. One morning at roll call in July, 1941, the guards discovered that prisoner #16670 had escaped. Actually, he had not escaped, but was sitting dead of starvation in the latrine. No one had had the strength to bring the corpse to the roll call, even though it was required by rule. It was further standard practice in the camp that, if anyone escaped, ten men from his barrack were automatically chosen at random to go to the Hunger Bunker, a series of cells in which prisoners stood without food until the escapee "returned."

One of the ten chosen fell to his knees, pleading, groveling, sobbing: "I have a wife and children." Fr. Kolbe calmly stepped forward and offered to take his place. The commandant, somewhat surprised at the offer, agreed.

For two weeks Max Kolbe stood in the Hunger Bunker, starving. Finally, on August 14, 1941, a doctor was sent in to give him a shot of strychnine. He had become an embarrassment.

Presidio Prison, San Francisco: Ricky Lee Todd had been in the stockade so long that he couldn't stand it any more—the sodomizing, the beatings, the filth, the sleepless fear. Five times he had attempted suicide (the Army called them "gestures"). On one occasion he cut his wrists when he was imprisoned in solitary. He was taken to the hospital where the wrists were sewn up and bandaged, and he was returned to the stockade. This time he re-moved the gauze from his wrists and hanged himself. When he arrived back at the hospital, he was pronounced dead but was revived. He had previously attempted suicide by slashing and hanging. After one of those earlier attempts, a guard hand-ed him a razor blade with the cheerful encouragement, "If you want to try again, here we go." After another, a guard squirted him with urine from a water pistol.

Pre-Test

1. The most humane way to treat the petty criminal is: (A) fine and probation;   (B) community service and probation;   (C) six months in state prison with a severe warning before probation.

2. Crime statistics indicate that the U.S. penal system: (A) is successful in rehabilitating most inmates;   (B) corrects and rehabilitates about half of all juvenile offenders;   (C) makes convicts worse than they were when sentenced.

3. The majority of inmates are: (A) rapists and murderers;   (B) small-time criminals;   (C) white collar criminals.

4. Torture and imprisonment for merely political differences is practiced today: (A) nowhere;   (B) only in the Soviet Union;   (C) in every military regime in South and Central America.

5. Military personnel who publicly protest army prisons are: (A) shot;   (B) turned over to impartial civilian courts;   (C) liable to the capital charge of mutiny.

6. The greatest contributing factor to petty crime, according to experts is: (A) rage and frustration;   (B) poverty and need;   (C) mental illness.

7. Former Vice President Spiro Agnew, found guilty on a charge of accepting bribes while in office as governor of Maryland: (A) pleaded no contest and was given probation and a fine;   (B) received the same sentence any other citizen would have received for the same crime;   (C) was impeached.

8. "Crimes of the poor" (robbery, car theft, etc.) amount each year to: (A) $2 billion;   (B) $600 million;   (C) $200 million.

9. "White collar crimes" (embezzlement, bribery, etc.) amount each year to: (A) $2 billion; (B) $600 million; (C) $200 million.

10. Of the thirty-nine hostages and inmates killed in the Attica uprising of 1971: (A) all were killed by inmates; (B) all were killed by state police; (C) none could be positively identified as killed by either side.

Almanac

1. In what United States city would you have the best chance of being:

Murdered _____

Raped _____

Burglarized _____

2. How many prisoners are in state and federal institutions?   2._____

3. What percentage are women?   3._____

4. What three states have the highest prison population in the United States?   4.(A)_____

(B)_____

(C)_____

5. What three states have the most men and women under sentence of death?   5.(A)_____

(B)_____

(C)_____

6. If each prisoner costs the taxpayer an average of about $30,000 a year, how much do state and federal prisons cost?   6._____

The Crime of Punishment

The famed psychiatrist, Dr. Karl Menninger, made a long study of crime and punishment. Here are some of his conclusions:

> Ninety percent of them (prisoners) have done no violence, and 80% of them could be handled more cheaply and effectively by other methods. But many of these wretches have illegally taken someone else's property, and this is a cardinal sin, tremendously important in a capitalistic society.
>
> We no longer cut off their hands, but we willingly spend $25-50,000 each to "punish," make miserable, and detain in idleness thieves whose illegal acquisitions—television sets, second-hand cars—could be bought for a few hundred dollars. The estimated national tax bill for making captured token offenders *suffer* (not for the arrest or trial or probation—just the squeeze) is over $1 billion annually! I doubt if the public is having that much fun from it. But that's what it is spending.
>
> Jails *ruin* young men. Can't the public grasp this indisputable fact? How can a decent prison attempting a rehabilitation program do anything for a boy who comes to it from a jail where he has been raped, battered, vomited and urinated upon, mauled, and corrupted by some of the oldtimers in the bullpen?

The President's Commission on Law Enforcement and Administration of Justice declared in 1967:

> Warring on poverty, inadequate housing and unemployment is warring on crime. A civil rights law is a law against crime. Money for schools is money against crime. Medical, psychiatric and family counseling services are services against crime. More broadly and most importantly, every effort to improve life in America's inner cities is an effort against crime.

President Richard Nixon, while still in office, said:

> Americans in the last decade were often told that the criminal was not responsible for his crimes against society, but that society was responsible. I totally disagree with this permissive philosophy. Society is guilty of crime only when we fail to bring the criminal to justice. When we fail to make the criminal pay for his crime, we encourage him to think that crime will pay. Such an attitude will never be reflected in the laws supported by this administration, nor in the manner in which we enforce those laws.

The McKay Commission, reporting on the Attica uprising, wrote:

> In the 1930's, New York State had a 98-day training course for prison guards. The program was progressive for its time, and older officers spoke highly of it. Between World War II and the late 1950's, however, there was no formal training for officers. More than one-third of the officers at Attica on September 9, 1971 [the day of the uprising], began their jobs during that period. Those who started after that were given two week's training . . . .
>
> With the exception of the Indian massacres in the late 19th century, the State Police assault which ended the four-day prison uprising was the bloodiest one-day encounter between Americans since the Civil War.
>
> Prison is the end of the criminal justice line—for inmates, for supervisory personnel, and for members of the public who have conveniently forgotten the institutions to which they abandon their most difficult fellow citizens. But official indifference and public forgetfulness is unacceptable. When society places a person behind walls, it cannot put aside its obligation to try to change and help that individual.

Role-Play

Vic Delaney has always been a good kid. A tough little football player with about average skill, a kind of hanger-on with a group, but genial, enjoyable. When you want help with a job, you can count on Vic.

Friday night, after the last senior exam and a week before graduation, Vic tagged along with the boys at a beer blast; and then, a bit tiddly, they all broke into school and, for a prank, pulled all the desks out of the first-floor classrooms and left them in the hall. Nothing else, just a bit of silliness. But Vic, who didn't hold his brew too well, was very giggly and uncharacteristically show-offish. He really loved the school and these guys, and to cover up his sadness, he "decided" on a prank of his own. "Hey, you guys, watch!" And he urinated on the assistant principal's door.

A few of the more sober called Vic several uncomplimentary names; and all of them, including the instantly sobered Vic, tried to clean up the mess. But they couldn't clean up inside the door. They had no key.

The next day, the assistant principal was furious and, through his grapevines, he discovered the entire story. He said that if that Delaney kid graduated onstage with the rest of the senior class, he was going to quit his job. Most of the faculty, knowing how their effectiveness depended on the assistant principal's effectiveness, backed him up. If he'd quit, they'd quit. But some believed that the punishment was too severe, that it overly penalized a kid who had never done anything serious before, as well as his parents who had waited four years for the graduation. It was making a mountain out of a molehill.

Role-Play
Faculty meeting to advise the principal what action to take. At the end, the principal decides.

Notebook Question

Page 14: It is almost certain that there is something going on in the United States today which you believe "somebody ought to do something about." (A) What is it for you? (B) Draft a very brief and tactful letter to your representative about that subject on this page of the notebook. [His or her name is listed in the Almanac, as is the address of the House of Representatives.]

Meditation

Love takes no pleasure in other people's sins, but delights in the truth. It is always ready to excuse, to trust, to hope, and to endure whatever comes.

—I Corinthians 13:6-7

When a sheriff or a marshal takes a man from a courthouse in a prison van and transports him to confinement for two or three or ten years, *this is our act.* We have tolled the bell for him. And whether we like it or not, we have made him our collective responsibility. We are free to do something about him; he is not.

—Chief Justice Warren Burger

Unit 15

The Poor in Body and Spirit

You don't know where
Your trouble is comin' from
But you know it's comin'
—Arthur Miller

Scottsboro, Georgia: Harold Cooper, his wife and four children inhabit a tumble-down house on a small patch of land in Georgia. They rent their acre-and-a-half for fifteen dollars a year, and their house for six dollars a month. They grow some of their own food, but they have no refrigeration. Mr. Cooper is in poor health and gets only occasional jobs. Mrs. Cooper needs an operation. The two youngest children are periodically treated for worms, a common problem when a family has no indoor plumbing. The worms are competing for what little nutrition Mrs. Cooper can give them.

Mrs. Cooper says that the reason they don't ask for food stamps is "the way you get treated there." The last ten days of the month, the family eats bread, syrup, and beans; but sometimes the beans don't hold out that long. The Cooper children often go hungry to school, even though the school offers lunches at the reduced price of 20 cents. When all four children can get to school, 80

cents is just too much; and Mrs. Cooper believes that the fairest way is to give none of them money.

———

Gary, Indiana: Edna Baines is 72, a widow of a steelworker who was laid off and never rehired. She has only her Social Security of $94.24 a week. "I wonder sometimes at the sounds I make," she says to herself. "Doesn't matter. Since Harry went, no one can hear them. My hands are all shriveled and spotty; the veins look like little blue snakes. Don't wear my teeth anymore; they got loose and clicked too much. After the long lonely night, awake most of the time so I won't soil the bed, I get up because, well, you got to have a routine.

"I like to sit in the window and feel the sun. The TV's broke. I don't go out. Don't trust the stairs. A boy from the high school comes once a week to buy groceries. Lord, I'd love to sit him down for an hour and just

let him talk. But he's shy and kindly. He sits awhile, but he's itching to get out and play ball. I suppose I frighten him a bit.

"I think maybe today, maybe today I can shut the two windows, and blow out the pilot light, and turn up the gas."

———

Vineland, New Jersey: Joseph Johnson was "slow." He did all right at his Daddy's farm, but the banks came and took that away and gave it to a big company. And his Daddy died. Joseph thought he died of shame. Joseph was very confused, wandering the streets of Hardin County, hoping that someone would notice him and give him work. One day another black man stopped him and offered him a job in the North. Joseph got onto a ramshackle old converted school bus and for two days traveled cramped in with many other ragged black men to New Jersey.

At the farm, they were crowded into chicken coops. The water they cooked with, drank, and bathed in came from a foul water tap that had been polluted by the nearby privy. Mostly they lived on stolen vegetables. There were a lot of flies. One lady let Joseph come with her children because he was simple. They slept six in a bed. There were a lot of roaches, too. And mosquitoes.

The men drank wine called "Tiger Rose" that they bought for a dollar a bottle from the black crew leaders who paid 50 cents for it. But Joseph didn't drink. His Daddy had told him not to. He liked the children better than the men. The children had fat, distended bellies; and they were infested with lice and ticks, but you got used to it. One night one of the children was bitten by a rat. But Joseph didn't know where else to go.

Pre-Test

Indicate the extent of your agreement or disagreement with the following.

1. Work should be the most important part of a person's life.	+ 2	+ 1	− 1	− 2
2. Success in an occupation is mainly a matter of knowing the right people.	+ 2	+ 1	− 1	− 2
3. It is better to be poor than to make a living by breaking the law.	+ 2	+ 1	− 1	− 2
4. Work is a good character builder.	+ 2	+ 1	− 1	− 2
5. One really shouldn't think well of himself unless he or she has a job.	+ 2	+ 1	− 1	− 2
6. The main satisfaction a person can get out of work is helping other people.	+ 2	+ 1	− 1	− 2
7. Welfare over a long time makes one feel cheap and ashamed.	+ 2	+ 1	− 1	− 2
8. To be truly successful in life, you have to care a lot about money.	+ 2	+ 1	− 1	− 2
9. I like work you can forget at the end of the day.	+ 2	+ 1	− 1	− 2
10. I like to work.	+ 2	+ 1	− 1	− 2

Almanac

A

The Bureau of Labor Statistics has developed what it calls a "less than adequate budget" for a family of four. Although it varies from state to state, in 1980 the average was $11,550. It was intended to be used only temporarily, and depended heavily on an ability to budget very carefully and get the most complete nutrition from the food section of that budget (skills which many in this bracket do not have).

1. If the family spent one-third on food, one-third for rent, and one-third for everything else, how much would they have in each of those thirds?

1._____

2. Divide that figure by fifty-two weeks.

2._____

3. How much of that final third would you personally allot for:

A. Transportation _____

B. Clothing _____

C. Personal care[1] _____

D. Medical _____

E. Other[2] _____

[1] Haircuts, insurance, cosmetics, cleaning, etc.
[2] Reading, recreation, tobacco, alcohol, education.

B

The Census Bureau has established a "Poverty Index" based on the assumption that most families spend one-third of their budgets on food (although many can't spend that much).

1. What is the Poverty Index this year for a family of four?

1._____

2. If the family spent one-third on food, one-third for rent, and one-third for everything else, how much would they have in each of those thirds?

2._____

3. Divide that figure by fifty-two weeks.

3._____

4. How much in that final third would you personally allot for:

A. Transportation _____

B. Clothing _____

C. Personal care _____

D. Medical _____

E. Other _____

C

1. How many persons this year does the government consider "officially poor," that is, below this year's poverty index?   1._____

2. What percentage is that of all Americans?   2._____

3. How many Americans are below the "less than adequate income" of $11,550?   3._____

4. What percentage is that of all Americans?   4._____

5. Of the total number of "officially poor," how many are children?   5._____

6. How many children receive AFDC?   6._____

7. What is the total amount spent on AFDC?   7._____

8. What is the budget of the Housing and Urban Development Department?   8._____

9. What is the budget of the Defense Dept.?   9._____

10. What are the total receipts of the United States government?   10._____

The Undeserving Poor

Stereotype	*Truth*
—Most of the poor are on welfare.	—Depends on where you draw the line on "poor." Only about a third of the poor receive any form of government assistance.
—Most of the men on welfare are able bodied loafers.	—The government puts the figure at about 1%.
—Most people on welfare are blacks and Puerto Ricans	—Of those on welfare, 56% are white; 31% are black; 11% are Hispanic; 2% are Asian; 1% are American Indian.
—Many people on welfare cheat.	—Government estimate: 4.9%, while tax experts estimate 33% of taxpayers cheat on their taxes: $200 billion every year.
—Welfare people live high.	—If two dollars per person a day for food is high off the hog, I don't know what the words mean.

Unemployment or underemployment among the poor are often due to forces that cannot be controlled by the poor themselves. The poor cannot be divided into those who will work and those who will not. For many, the desire to work is strong, but the opportunities are not. Generally, the poor are doing what they can, considering their age, health status, social circumstances, location, education, and opportunities for employment. Poverty is not a chosen way of life.

—*Presidential Commission on Poverty*

Persons should regard their lawful possessions not merely as their own but also as common property, in the sense that they should benefit not only themselves but others.

For the rest, the right to have a share of earthly goods sufficient for oneself and one's family belongs to everyone. The Fathers and Doctors of the church held this view, teaching that persons are obliged to come to the relief of the poor, and to do so not merely out of their superfluous goods. If a person is in extreme necessity, such a one has the right to take from the riches of others what he or she needs.

Since there are so many people in this world afflicted with hunger, this sacred Council urges all, both individuals and governments, to remember the saying of the Fathers: "Feed those dying of hunger, because if you have not fed them you have murdered them."

—*Vatican Council II,* The Church Today

Out of these new conditions of society the baseless theory unfortunately emerged which considered profit the key motive for economic progress, competition as the supreme law of economics, and private ownership of the means of production as an absolute right that has no limits and carries no corresponding social obligations. This unchecked liberalism led to dictatorship rightly denounced by Pius XI as producing "the international imperialism of money." One cannot condemn such abuses too strongly, because—let us again recall solemnly—the economy should be at the service of man.

—Pope Paul VI

Every gun that is made, every warship launched, every rocket fired signifies, in the final sense, a theft from those who hunger and are not fed, those who are cold and are not clothed.

—Dwight D. Eisenhower

Role-Play

Otis Wilmot had been a hotshot all his life. In a sense, he had to be in order to survive. He and his younger brothers had spent their tender years stomping cockroaches and clubbing rats in their tenement. They each had different fathers, men they had never seen. Their mother was a kindly woman, hardworking, but she said that at times she just "got lonely," and Otis understood that.

Otis graduated from rat patrol to store patrol; and after several warnings from the local policemen about shoplifting food, he finally got caught in a store and, just after he had punched out a clerk, was arrested.

He was sent to Rahway Prison for a session which the lifers had developed for juvenile offenders and which has been publicized in the film *Scared Straight.* Well, it scared Otis all right. He vowed never again to take a chance that might land him in that place. He vowed he was going to get a job and get his family off welfare and out of that hellhole.

Well, he tried. But Otis had automatically been passed from grade to grade by teachers whose main job was maintaining order. Everyplace he tried, it was either "No openings," or $1.28 an hour. His mother said it was better than nothing, but Otis couldn't stand it. He had to get out of that place. Not in ten years. Now. So, Otis made a new vow: either he was going to get a job that didn't treat him like a slave, or he was going to pull off a big job and lam out of town, or he was going to kill himself. One of the three.

Role-Play
—Otis with his probation officer (who has 120 clients)
—Otis and his three younger brothers
—A group therapy session in which Otis's vow is the subject. Other members: a former teenage prostitute, a former heroin addict, a former alcoholic, a former numbers runner, and a non-directive group leader.

Notebook Question

Page 15: Suppose the government sent you the money you needed to live at the "less than adequate" level mentioned in the unit, and that you could keep the grant whether you worked or not. Would you work or not? Give your reasons.

Meditation

Do not forget: thin sowing means thin reaping. The more you sow, the more you reap. Each one should give what he has decided in his own mind, not grudgingly or because he is made to, for God loves a cheerful giver. And there is no limit to the blessing which God can send you. He will make sure that you will always have what you need for yourselves in every possible circumstance, and you will still have something to spare for all sorts of good works. As scripture says: he was free in almsgiving, and gave to the poor: his good deeds will never be forgotten.

—II Corinthians 9:6-9

After eighty years of modern social teachings and over two thousand years of the gospel of love, the church has to admit her inability to make more impact on the conscience of her people. The faithful, particularly the more wealthy and comfortable, simply do not see structured social justice as a sin, and they feel no personal responsibility for it. To live like Dives with Lazarus at the gate is not even perceived to be sinful.

—The Roman Synod, 1971

Unit 16

Our World Neighborhood's Poor

Send not to know for whom the bell tolls.
It tolls for thee.
—*John Donne*

Calcutta, India: Lal Singh was born in the south, in Bangalore, thirty-two years ago. He was an indifferent student as a boy, but he managed to get a good job as an assistant in a small forge. He married and has two children. Two years ago, however, while trying to unclog ash in the old boiler of the forge, he inadvertently pressed his hand against the hot boiler plate. The flesh seared, but Lal Singh felt no pain. He was not a man of learning, but he knew at once what it was. Somehow, although he bathed once a week, he had become a leper.

He spoke to no one but left work. The children were in school, and his wife was working. He went to the cupboard and took out of the small tin tea box one half of their savings. He left a note saying that he had left for another woman. Better that his neighbors believe his wife had been deserted than that she and the children also be driven out. As he left, he took the small bell his wife used to summon the children.

Strangers on the road must be warned he was coming.

Ribeiraio Bonito, Brazil: Santana Paredes came from a shantytown in Recife to the backlands of Brazil to escape the squalor, the degradation, and the threats of the police death squads. She was seventeen when she escaped the whorehouse where she had been sent by her mother in order to get some food for the other seven brothers and sisters. She had paid her debt to her family every night for two years, and then she had fled to the "Wild West." She was going to start new and clean again.

But there is a saying: "A new sky above your head does not change the soul within you." Santana now works in a whorehouse in a little dun-colored town in a wide space along Federal Highway BR-158. The men come into town on Saturday to drink and brawl and tumble the

whores, brutally. They have no more money than she. They work on the *fazendas* for dirt and pay most of their wages back to the bosses for food and lodging. The few *cruzeiros* they have left over, they send home to their families to fend off death for one more month.

Each town is a place of indifference. Each person is a sack of indifference. But one goes on. As long as there is food. One faces the drunken stranger because he means food. When there are no more strangers and no more food? Santana will think of that later.

Kigali, Rwanda: Francois Hutu is called "Reynard" because he is so clever. He is eighteen and works for Mme. Sophie Giraux, the white mistress of the Minister of the Exchequer. She is also in the pay both of the Americans and of the Russians to relay to them the "state secrets" of Rwanda. Francois is also in the pay of the French and East Germans to tell them all he knows of the great doings of state he might overhear. Each month he makes up stories and says he has overheard them while the minister was dallying with his mistress. It means a few francs each month which Francois sends home to his family in the bush. In fact,"Reynard" also keeps several families in the capital alive with the garbage of Mme. Giraux and the minister.

Pre-Test

1.   If Lal Singh were to look for a doctor to diagnose his symptoms in India, his chances of finding one would be less than: (A) 1/100;   (B) 12/1000;   (C) 26/100,000;   (D) 30/1,000,000.

2.   In Brazil where Santana Paredes lives, by what percentage do consumer prices rise each year?   (A) 6.9%;   (B) 10.8%;   (C) 50%;   (D) 95%.

3.   What percentage of its Gross National Product does the United States give away each year in foreign aid?   (A) .2%;   (B) .5%; (C) 1%;   (D) 5%.

4.   What percentage of its Gross National Product does Sweden, by law, give away each year in foreign aid?   (A) .2%;   (B) .5%; (C) 1%;   (D) 5%.

5.   How many companies in the United States do the Japanese hold a controlling interest in?   (A) 10;   (B) 50;   (C) 150;   (D) 225.

6.   Of the twenty-eight banks in California, how many are foreign-owned?   (A) 3;   (B) 5;   (C) 7;   (D) 10.

7.   Outright, no-strings grants to underdeveloped foreign countries are good for the United States because: (A) it is the humanitarian thing to do;   (B) it is the Christian thing to do;   (C) it is in the self-interest of the United States;   (D) all of the above.

8. More than one out of ten children die in infancy in: (A) Angola; (B) Benin; (C) Bolivia; (D) Burundi; (E) Cape Verde; (F) Central African Republic; (G) Chad; (H) Congo; (I) Egypt; (J) Ethiopia; (K) Gabon; (L) Gambia; (M) Ghana; (N) Guinea; (0) Guinea-Bissau; (P) Honduras; (Q) India; (R) Ivory Coast; (S) Lesotho; (T) Liberia; (U) Madagascar; (V) Malawi; (W) Maldives; (X) Mali; (Y) Mauritania; (Z) Morocco; (AA) Mozambique; (BB) Niger; (CC) Pakistan; (DD) Rwanda; (EE) Senegal; (FF) Sudan; (GG) Swaziland; (HH) Tanzania; (II) Togo; (JJ) Uganda; (KK) Upper Volta; (LL) South Yemen; (MM) Zaire; (NN) Zambia; (00) Zimbabwe; (PP) all of the above.

9. In what country is the Infant Mortality Rate per 1,000 listed as "Africans-94, Asians-25.3, Whites-14.9"? (A) U.S.; (B) U.S.S.R.; (C) China; (D) South Africa.

10. Despite the fact that there is war going on there, which of the following is among the top ten fastest growing populations in the world? (A) El Salvador; (B) Honduras; (C) Iraq; (D) all of the above.

Almanac

1. How many persons in the Far East are below the Critical Minimum Food limit each day?   1._____

2. Of all the "undeveloped" nations of Africa, Latin America, the Near and Far East, how many are below the daily calorie requirements?   2._____

3. According to the most recent statistics, how many refugees are there in the world?   3._____

4. What is by far the most widely spoken language in the world?   4._____

5. What are the three largest cities in the world, by population?

5.(A)_____

(B)_____

(C)_____

6. What country has the most people per square mile (10,700 per square mile)?

6._____

7. Under the title "U.S. Foreign Trade," what is the year's dollar value of United States exports and imports with the following countries?

	Exports	Imports
Japan	_____	_____
West Germany	_____	_____
United Kingdom	_____	_____
Red China	_____	_____
Nigeria	_____	_____

8. Is there any major trade area in the world with which the United States has a favorable balance of trade (i.e., exports exceed imports)?

8._____

9. What was the profit/loss ratio for the United States in world trade last year?

9._____

10. On what single item is the United States most dependent for outside imports?

10._____

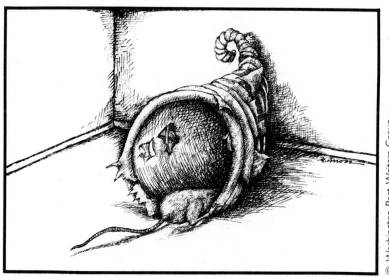

© Washington Post Writers Group

123

Starvation

The victim of starvation burns up his own body fats, muscles, and tissues for fuel. His body quite literally consumes itself and deteriorates rapidly. The kidneys, liver, and endocrine system often cease to function properly. A shortage of carbohydrates, which play a vital role in brain chemistry, affects the mind. Lassitude and confusion set in, so that starvation victims often seem unaware of their plight. The body's defenses drop, disease kills most famine victims before they have time to starve to death. An individual begins to starve when he has lost about a third of his normal body weight. Once this loss exceeds 40%, death is inevitable.

—*TIME, 1 Nov 74*

What comfort is it to an Indian peasant, whose baby is likely to starve, to be told that the bins of Canada are bursting and that India herself is capable of producing ten times as much food as she is producing? What can she do about it? What can the dweller in a Glasgow slum do to break down restrictive practices and trade barriers without which, she is told, there would be an abundance for all? She wants to know what she may do here and now in a world in which doubtless many foolish practices are pursued, but over which she has no control. What use is it to tell the people of Barbados to be fruitful and multiply and that the world is not overcrowded? Barbados is overcrowded, and they are in Barbados.

—*Christopher Hollis*

When one has had a great deal given him, a great deal will be required of him.

—*Luke 12:48*

Warn those who are rich in this world's goods that they are not to look down on other people; and not set their hopes on money, which is untrustworthy, but on God who, out of his riches, gives us all that we need for our happiness. Tell them that they are to do good, and be rich in good works, to be generous and willing to share—this is the way they can save up a good capital sum for the future if they want to make sure of the only life that is real.

—*I Timothy 6:17-19*

Five Commandments

1. Thou shalt not become cynical.
2. Thou shalt not become liberally guilt complexed.
3. Thou shalt not wait for the dramatic opportunity.
4. Thou shalt not underestimate thyself.
5. Thou shalt find one cause, and crusade for it.

Addresses for the following are right there in the Almanac:

Big Brothers/Big Sisters of America

Bread for the World

CARE

National Council of Catholic Bishops

Child Welfare League of America

Common Cause

American Association of Correctional Officers

Foreign Policy Association

Federation of the Handicapped

Americans for Human Rights and Social Justice

American Leprosy Missions

Literacy Volunteers of America

March of Dimes

Birth Defects Foundation

Muscular Dystrophy Association

NAACP

Negro College Fund

National Society for Shut-Ins

Social Service

UNICEF

National Organization for Women

Women's Overseas Service League

Everybody has a hobby. Why not make your hobby people?

Role-Play

Choose five people to be policymakers for the United States. They have decided to emulate Sweden and give, from their abundance, 1% of the country's GNP (1% of $2.6 trillion). Everybody else in the room is the representative of an undeveloped country. (See "Nations of the World.") He or she knows all the information the Almanac provides about GNP, per capita income, infant mortality, and so on. Let each plead his or her case, and let the policymakers divide the grants and decide whether they want to attach any strings to them.

Notebook Question

Page 16: The purpose of this book has been to make you aware of a whole rabbit warren of injustices, here at home and around the world. It was also intended to make you aware that, even though you are young, even though you are only one person, even though you might feel powerless, you are not powerless. You can't crusade for everything, but as a Christian you have to crusade for something. What?

Meditation

Lord, grant me the serenity to accept the things that can't be changed, the courage to change the things that can be changed, and the wisdom to know the difference. Amen.